Is that Billing…p?

Tottie Limejuice

The sequel to *Sell the Pig*.

CreateSpace Independent Publishing Platform, 2013.

Foreword

Is That Billinge Lump? is the second in a proposed trilogy of memoirs, plus a prequel, about a dysfunctional family's move to France in search of a better life. In particular, it's about the search for better healthcare for my ninety-year-old mother who suffered from vascular dementia.

Billinge Lump, like the first part, *Sell the Pig*, is a true story, told as accurately as I can, without exaggeration or embellishment. I've tried to write the sequel as a stand-alone for those who have not yet read *Sell the Pig*, whilst not wanting to repeat myself to those who have.

So I'll try to summarise *Sell the Pig* here as briefly as possible. If you've already read *Sell the Pig*, you can skip this bit.

Mother had reached eighty-nine and was getting steadily more frail and gaga, with what used to be called senile dementia. We'd had some fairly horrendous experiences of her living at home with the supposed support of carers visiting daily, before moving her into a succession of homes. We started with care homes, then moved up to the more intense level of nursing care.

Success had been mixed. The very best home was wonderful, but as a care home, couldn't provide the increased level of nursing care she needed. It was time to do something drastic.

In one of those 'it seemed like a good idea at the time' moments, I suggested to my brother we should all move to France together and buy a large enough house for all of us to share, so we could tap into one of Europe's best healthcare systems.

On the downside, my brother and I have never got on terribly well, and he suffers equally from depression and alcohol addiction, with the vicious circle that entails. I thought he might do better in France, and his depression might be helped by living with Mother of whom he was extremely fond.

So after much house-hunting, my brother signed the contract for what we called the Pink House, in central France's Auvergne region. One March day in 2007, we loaded Mother, with two nurses to ensure she was safe and well on the journey, into my brother's Hymer motorhome, known affectionately as The Dingley, and headed for the Channel Tunnel.

I followed behind in my battered old Vauxhall Combo van, taking with me my beloved collie, Meic, (pronounced Mike), who was also elderly and suffered from a heart condition.

Me? I'm an eccentric middle-aged freelance copywriter, far too optimistic for my own good, who thought we could be heading for a better life for all of us. All this despite the fact that all the staff in the nursing home were convinced we would kill Mother off before we even crossed the Severn Bridge out of Wales.

Sell the Pig ended as we arrived in France. *Is That Billinge Lump?* takes up the story from there.

Chapter One
Settling In

That feeling. When you open your eyes and have absolutely no idea at all where you are. Despite my body clock being sure it was daytime, the room was as black as pitch. My eyes seemed to be functioning as normal, but when I blinked them rapidly a few times, it was still dark.

Then I remembered. Yesterday I had arrived in France, to start a new life. The blackness was because my room in my brother's house had wooden shutters, which were still closed. We called the house the Pink House, because it had looked delightfully rosy in the estate agent's print-out, though had since faded to a grubby washed-out shade, like when you accidentally put something red in with your white undies.

I couldn't locate a light switch near the bed in the darkness of an unfamiliar room so I scrambled out of bed, or rather up from the mattress on the floor on which I had slept during the night, my own cabin bed not yet having been put together. My elderly collie Meic (pronounced Mike) was still sleeping the slumber of a dog who'd spent thirteen hours the day before in my blue Vauxhall van driving down from Calais to our new home in Central France's Auvergne.

I stumbled across to where I thought the window might be, managed to fumble it open, and flung open the shutters. What was to be my new bedroom for the foreseeable future faced east and already the morning sunlight was coming streaming in on what looked like a beautiful day.

Time to check on the reason for the relocation. In the next bedroom to mine was my eighty-nine-year-old mother who, with two nurses to take care of her en route, had yesterday travelled down through France in a motorhome, affectionately known as The Dingley, being driven by my brother, a part-time alcoholic with bi-polar disorder.

Against all the odds, and against the advice of countless people who thought we were absolutely, certifiably mad, we had decided to uproot Mother from the UK and bring her over to France. We were looking for a better quality of life, and in particular, a better quality of care.

Mother had vascular dementia. What used to be called 'going a bit senile' or 'a bit gaga'. She didn't have Alzheimer's disease, thankfully, but she most certainly no longer had all her marbles. Her short-term memory was reduced to seconds, a minute or two at best. Yet she still remembered all the poems of her youth, which she happily recited several dozen times a day. And she always knew who I was.

I tapped on her bedroom door and went in. The two nurses, one from an agency, the other from the nursing home where Mother had been living before making the move, had her up, washed and dressed and were just finishing tidying her hair.

For someone of eighty-nine, with a weak heart, and countless other medical conditions as well as her dementia, who all of the nurses and carers at the home told us would never survive a one thousand mile journey by road and channel tunnel shuttle, she looked remarkably bright. She beckoned me imperiously with a wave of her hand.

"This is my daughter," she said to the two nurses, rather as if she were presenting me at court, although of course they knew who I was.

Mother was always a bit of a character, even when playing with a full deck of cards. A wicked sense of humour caused some hilarious situations with her almost child-like way of saying exactly what she thought.

On one memorable occasion, I had taken her, together with my best friend Jill, to stay in an apartment on the Costa de la Luz in southern Spain. It was the first anniversary of my father's death and, being the beginning of November, it was cold, wet and dismal in Stockport where Mother lived, so I thought a change of scene and some sunshine would be just the thing.

We were eating in a nice seafood restaurant which Jill and I had discovered on our visit to the area the previous year. It was unpretentious, not expensive, and served fish so fresh you could taste the tang of the Atlantic.

The decoration consisted of an inset area in the centre of the floor, filled with pots and pots of plants and greenery, which always looked a little dusty.

As the waiter was passing our table, Mother said to me: "Tell that young man his aspidistras need dusting."

I looked at the impossibly tight-trousered, pert-buttocked young man who was waiting expectantly, sensing that a remark was about to be addressed to him. And I thought, even if I had the Spanish vocabulary, I was not going to risk saying: "My mother wants to dust your aspidistras".

On the first full day of our new life in France, we all assembled in the kitchen for breakfast, after I'd taken patient old Meic for a quick walk to stretch his legs and relieve himself.

My brother was up and in good form, always a bit of a gamble, given his alcohol dependence. But one good thing about him is that he almost never drinks when driving. He'd stayed sober for the whole drive over, which had taken us two days in total as he was navigating and always prefers the scenic route to avoid motorways. As the agency nurse was returning home that day and he was driving her to the airport, he had stayed sober again.

They set off for the airport, taking the other nurse with them, as she'd been promised some time off to visit the area. I managed to manhandle Mother and her wheelchair out of what the English call French windows but the French more logically call door windows, onto the sunny south-facing patio. I then wheeled her a little way up the lawned area so she could see the magnificent view.

We had arrived in the Puy de Dôme *département* of central France's Auvergne region. From the house, we looked down onto the very fertile Limagne plain. In one of life's strange coincidences, as a copywriter in Lincolnshire, I'd once written for a client who worked there, without ever knowing exactly where it was.

We couldn't actually see the iconic landmark of the region, the Puy de Dôme volcano, from the house, but several others were visible, as were the mountains of the Forez chain, away to the east. Mother looked at one of the cone shaped volcanoes and asked: "Is that Billinge Lump?"

Billinge Lump is the local name for Billinge Hill, the highest point of Mother's native St Helens, in what used to be Lancashire but has now merged into Merseyside. It was a favourite place for us to go for picnics when we visited Mother's mother, her elder sister and one of her brothers, who all lived together on Bleak Hill, Eccleston.

Granny used to love to take us up Billinge Lump in blackberry season to pick the berries to make delicious jam and pies. She was always outraged if anyone else had had the temerity to go up there before us and would roundly curse the 'thieving pickers' who'd been up and stripped the bushes of the best berries. Although of course they had as much right to nature's bounty as we did.

My brother and I had decided not to tell Mother that she had moved to France for good. We weren't sure if she was even capable of taking the information on board, with the impairment to her mental faculties. She would almost certainly forget five minutes after we told her, but in the short term, we decided it might upset her. We had agreed instead to tell her that we were on holiday in France, which she could certainly understand and would probably enjoy.

I explained this to her and pointed out the lovely warm sunshine and the beautiful view from where we were.

"Oh, that's nice," she said, then immediately pointed to another one of the small volcanoes and asked again: "Is that Billinge Lump?"

Yes, Mother. To you, it probably is.

It was pleasantly warm in contrast to chilly and damp Wales which we had left just two days ago. Small brown lizards were starting to appear on the patio and on the walls of the Pink House. One in particular stopped on the crazy paving close to Mother's wheelchair and paused to look at her in that intense, inscrutable way reptiles have. It lifted its feet one at a time, a trick they have which apparently stops them from getting too hot.

Mother exclaimed in delight. "Oh look," she said, "it's waving to me!" and proceeded to chirrup away and wave back to the lizard in the same way she loved to chirrup to the birds in the garden.

One of the first things we needed to sort out in our new home and lifestyle was some help for me to get Mother in and out of her bed, mornings and evenings. She had never been large and was now even smaller as osteoporosis slowly reduced her spine, but she was still a dead weight and my neck had never fully recovered from a whiplash injury inflicted by a horse.

Mother also had a habit, whenever I helped her anywhere, of letting me take most of her weight. She would make much more effort to help herself for nurses and carers. I assume it was a measure of her trust in me not to drop her.

The second nurse was going home in a couple of days and I was definitely going to need help.

I was being my characteristically optimistic self in assuming I could slip seamlessly into a life of tending to Mother's every need, which included toileting and coping with not infrequent little accidents. I'd never even babysat for anyone, let alone had children of my own, but, being an eternal optimist, I was sure I could manage. Even I should have realised it was going to involve a steep learning curve.

My brother had arranged for two people from home care service providers to come and visit to see which, if either, would be suitable for Mother's needs. One was a very attractive young woman who spent a lot of time going over the figures, explaining to us exactly what the service would cost, what was provided and how the system worked.

The other was older, perhaps in her forties, and I immediately mentally nicknamed her Hippy Chick. She had bright henna red hair under a floppy purple velvet hat, an impossibly short skirt, a long mohair sweater and biker boots. She insisted on meeting Mother, made an instant connection with her, spoke to her in passable English, having lived for some time in the Far East, and discussed at great length Mother's needs and how they could best be met. She mentioned her fees almost in passing; they were about three times that of the other service.

My brother voted for the good looking one. I voted for Hippy Chick. In the end I won, as a better life for Mother was largely what the move had all been about.

Those first few days were idyllic for all of us. The weather was unbelievable, day after day of clear blue skies and warm sunshine. The garden was bursting into life and birds were singing as they claimed their territory. Every day I was able to take Mother out into the garden and park her wheelchair in the sunshine so she could watch the birds and wave to the lizards while I made a start at some gardening, as there was a lot to do.

And every day Mother would point to the nearest volcano and ask: "Is that Billinge Lump?"

I didn't go out and about, apart from three short walks a day with Meic, morning and evening when Hippy Chick was seeing to Mother and a quick nip out at lunchtime whilst Mother was snoozing. I quickly discovered the local people were very friendly and would always call a polite greeting and be happy to pass the time of day.

My French still needed work, of course, and would often get me into tricky situations with me either saying the wrong word or misunderstanding what was said to me. One day I was weeding around the splendid silver birch tree halfway up the steps to the patio from the front gate, preparing to plant some grape hyacinths.

A group of people were walking past and we exchanged *bonjours*, then one of them made a comment, in a sympathetic tone, about the birch tree, or so I thought. I smiled politely and nodded in agreement, wondering if there was some local superstition that meant birches were unlucky.

It was only later, when I heard the word again in another context, that I realised he had said *boulot*, or work, not *bouleau* or birch tree, as the two words sound practically identical. What he was actually saying was 'you've got some work on', referring to the size of garden I was tackling, and not 'oh dear, you've got a birch tree'!

My brother was in very good form in those early days. Since he loves shopping and I hate it, he was in charge of going out for provisions. Most of the time he did the cooking too, both of which gave him an incentive to stay sober.

He would buy the papers, including the English ones, albeit a day late, and sit in the sunshine to read them, next to Mother.

Mother was visibly flourishing with all the individual attention, the beautiful weather and, above all, plenty to drink to avoid dehydration and urinary infections. We were still treated to all her favourite sayings and poems, trotted out whenever there was the slightest lull in conversation, or particularly when attention was switched away from her for any reason.

Early on, we had the local mayor and his wife round for afternoon tea, for which my brother baked scones, being a very good pastry cook who had learned catering in his Navy days. Mr and Mrs Mayor ran a B&B in their *chateau* just up the road and my brother had stayed there a few times when he was completing the sale on the Pink House. He had decided they were his new best friends.

He's not always very good at the rules of engagement of friendship. I'm much more cynical and couldn't help wondering if their interest in us was more the three potential votes in the next municipal election rather than any genuine interest in or friendship with us as individuals.

I was particularly dubious of their motives when early on, they took my brother for a drive round the village pointing out who was who and who lived where and telling him rather more than I thought proper for a mayor to say about his townsfolk.

Hippy Chick was turning out to be absolutely marvellous. Whenever she came, there was a lot of chatting and laughing coming from Mother's room. Mother would often arrive in the kitchen for breakfast wearing one or another of Hippy Chick's collection of funky hats, or one of her rings or bracelets. She had become a real magpie as she got older, always wanting anything bright and shiny that anyone else was wearing.

Within a week of arriving at the Pink House, it was Mother's birthday. She was ninety years old, though looked younger, and with the effects of the sun, constant stimulation and plenty of good food, she was starting to look better every day.

When I went into her bedroom on her birthday with her morning cup of tea, I told her it was her birthday.

"Is it?" she asked. "How old am I?"

When I told her, she immediately said: "I'm not! Ninety? I never am. Ninety my bum!" Bum was a word of which she had become extremely fond as she got older.

"How old do you think you are?" I asked.

"Twenty-one," she replied, and began to sing: "I'm twenty-one today, twenty-one today. I've got the key of the door, I've never been twenty-one before. And Father says I can do as I like, so I shouted Hip-hooray! Da-da-da-da-da-da-dah-da (where she'd forgotten the line), Twenty-one today."

Memory really is a curious thing. Just about all of Mother's memory of the last thirty or forty years had disappeared. She had lost all ability to learn or remember anything new. But she could still dredge up songs and poems from her childhood and recite them more or less perfectly. She and Hippy Chick were already comfortably exchanging 'See you later, alligator', 'In a while, crocodile,' on their daily encounters.

Sometimes Mother would surprise me, and herself, and come out with a word or expression that was on a much higher level than her usual daily patter. One day we sat on the lawn drinking in the views, having done the ritual exchange of: "Is that Billinge Lump?", "No, Mother, we're in France. On holiday." She looked down at the small town on the plain and asked: "Is that an agglomeration? I want to say agglomeration, but I don't know if it's the right word."

Mother loved to be outside and now she could be, whenever it was fine. I know older people have fragile skin but I always smothered her in high protection sun cream and put on her hat and sunglasses. And after all, she was ninety years old; slowly developing skin cancer was probably the least of her worries.

Her hands no longer worked very well but she had always loved gardening so I got her to advise me on what to prune and plant and even got her doing little housework jobs to the best of her ability. I'd give her a duster and bring small pieces of furniture across for her to polish, or get her to help clean the silver.

The transformation in a short time was quite incredible. In the home, she had been on anti-depressants. Now she was full of laughter again and clearly having more fun than she'd had in years.

One of her favourite expressions when she was amused was 'Eeeeh, yaff laff.'

Mother came from 'oop north', born and bred in St Helens in Lancashire, where they do, often, say 'eeeeeh', though never 'bah gum.' When she was young, one of the neighbours, who had a broad Lancashire accent, always used to say 'yaff laff' which, translated for anyone not from 'oop north', was the local way of saying 'you have to laugh'.

It had been a long time since she had done any walking. As she had become more frail and had had a few falls in the nursing home, the management there were no longer prepared to allow her to try to walk, as they simply did not have sufficient staff to give her the support she needed.

Hippy Chick and I were determined to get her mobile again and soon had her walking the short distance between her bedroom, the kitchen and the sitting room, using her walking frame and supported by one or both of us. I even had her doing a few steps in the garden when she and I were by ourselves for the day, though that was more difficult because of the uneven surface.

For some strange reason, whenever we were helping her to walk anywhere, she would always start singing 'Here comes the bride', or rather, as she had forgotten those words, just singing 'da-da-da-da' to the right tune.

We now had English television via Freesat, so on the very rare occasions when the weather was not perfect for Mother to be outside, she could sit in front of her favourite daytime TV shows like 'Cash in the Attic', 'Bargain Hunt' and 'To Buy or Not to Buy', with the subtitles on so she could follow what was happening.

The phone line was now connected and we had an Internet connection, so I could carry on my work as a freelance copywriter, for my clients in the UK, and safely leave Mother half an hour or so at a time whilst I worked in the next room. I found I couldn't work in the same room as, even with the subtitles on, Mother liked the television turned up very loud which made it impossible for me to concentrate.

Everything was working out as well, if not better, than we had hoped for when we decided to make the move to France.

Even an optimist like me, however, realised that it couldn't last. Sooner or later the weather would break, literally and figuratively. I was after all sharing living space with a mother with vascular dementia and an alcoholic brother with manic depressive symptoms. Something was bound to go bang eventually.

The catalyst, somewhat unexpectedly, was the visit of some old and very dear friends from the UK. And what actually precipitated the eruption, when it came, was a seemingly innocent bowl of lettuce.

Chapter Two
Explosive Lettuce

Bob and Peg had been my very good friends since the 1970s. I first met them when I was working on a newspaper in South Wales. A young work experience girl called Janey came to work with me in the newsroom and we became friends . She introduced me to Bob and Peg as she was going out with their youngest son.

The newspaper I worked on that time, a local weekly, was privately owned and run on a bit of a shoestring budget, which is why young people on work experience sometimes found themselves doing jobs above their level of competence.

Publication day on local newspapers is always somewhat nail-biting. Soon after the papers hit the shelves, there would be the inevitable phone calls to the newsroom complaining about every minor typographical error, names misspelled, vital names missing from reports and quibbles over facts.

I was nearest to the phone on one particular publication day and when I answered the call, I was more than a little surprised when a man asked: "Can you tell me, since when has the penalty for illegal parking been so severe?"

Somewhat nervously I turned to the offending page number he mentioned and read for myself. The first paragraph was harmless enough, the name and address of the driver, the fine, the court and the date of the court appearance.

With a sickening feeling in the pit of my stomach, I started to read the following paragraph: 'The magistrates ordered that the defendant should be hanged, drawn and quartered and his remains dragged through the town square by Red Rum.'

Oops.

Hastily assuring the man on the phone that there had clearly been some mistake (nothing like stating the obvious) I reported to our chief sub editor what had happened and he did some investigating.

This was still in the days of hot metal presses, and it transpired that one of the linotype operators seriously fancied another young work experience girl who had been given the job of checking the galley proofs. These were the first proofs to come off the presses and theoretically, shouldn't contain many errors. The copy had already been checked by a sub editor and provided the linotype operator was not careless, there should be few mistakes.

If any errors were detected, it was the job of the person checking the galley proofs to take them back to the linotype operator to request correction. The young lad thought that if he made such a glaring change to the copy, the girl would have to come over and talk to him about it and he might then be able to pluck up the courage to ask her out.

Unfortunately, for reasons known best to herself, the girl had checked the offending paragraph for spelling errors and, not finding any, had let it through.

It was also on that same newspaper where I drew the short straw one day and was despatched to interview Jimmy Savile when he made a visit to the town. And the interview took place in what he called his 'shag wagon', the motorhome in which he toured the country and which was parked on the town car park whilst he visited. I did survive with my virtue, such as it was, intact. However his pawing, over-familiar behaviour towards me led me to say for evermore that nothing whatsoever which came to light about him in the future would surprise me.

But back to Bob and Peg, our first visitors coming to stay since our arrival in France. I was hugely looking forward to seeing them, they were very great friends, and I thought it would be nice, too, for Mother, as she had known them and become friends with them through me. I thought some extra company would be stimulating for her.

They were of a similar age to my parents. Bob was exactly the same age as Mother but had weathered the years very much better, with only some impaired hearing to show for his ninety years. He was still as mentally sharp as ever, demonstrated by the fact that their visit to us was to be made on their way back from visiting friends in Spain, with Bob doing all the driving, all the way from South Wales where they still lived.

Peg was a piano teacher and I'd often been a visitor to their house for her musical *soirées*. They always ended with everyone crowded round the piano while she played, all of us singing a wide variety of songs, from old Welsh favourites like *'Calon Lân'* and *'Ar Lan y Môr'* to Irish songs like 'Down By the Salley Gardens'.

They were the only friends in whom I would tolerate unpunctuality, which is a bit of a bugbear of mine. A few minutes late is excusable; Bob and Peg's record on one occasion was more than two hours late for dinner. I forgave them because, as I stood on the doorstep of the smallholding in Wales where I lived at that time, I could see the lights of their car driving forlornly round and round the nearby lanes and just not finding the driveway to my house. Those were the days long before mobile phones and with no public telephone box for miles around.

They were also the only people on whom I could call at very strange times of the night and still find them up and receiving guests. And where any invitation to a meal was always an interesting experience – when I once took Mother for Sunday lunch, Peg didn't even start to prepare anything till after three in the afternoon.

Bob was slightly built and still looked athletic. He was passionate about tennis and still queued and camped out to get his tickets for Wimbledon, and was once interviewed by the BBC as the oldest spectator doing so.

Peg, although younger, seemed to be ageing faster and had not fared as well as Bob, but was still as bright and amusing as ever. She had a delightful sense of humour and could recite some of the filthiest limericks I've ever heard in such a way as to render them completely inoffensive and extremely funny.

Just to give you a flavour, I'll quote what is probably her least *risqué*. But first you need to picture a rather short and well built elderly lady, with thinning hennaed hair and her reading glasses hanging off one ear. Beautifully spoken, with an open, smiling face and wickedly twinkling eyes.

Perhaps imagine Madame Cholet from the Wombles, with just a tad more mischief about her. Confusingly, the French word for mischief is *malice*. And although there was never any malice to Peg's humour, it was certainly well on the naughty side of mischief, as shown by her most presentable limerick:

'There was a young man from Aberystwyth
Took his girlfriend home to play whist with.
But instead of that,
They sat on the mat,
And played with the things that they pissed with.'

Bob and Peg were intrepid travellers, borne out by their marathon drive, which would have been taxing for people half their age. Both got by quite adequately in French, although Bob could rival me on the making mistakes with words front, perhaps his best to date being stopping and asking someone the way to the war (*guerre*) instead of the railway station (*gare*).

My brother and I had chosen the Pink House out of all the ones we had looked at because the top storey had a very pleasant, light and airy suite. There were three bedrooms with a shower, loo and room for a kitchen/dining area, which would be ideal for our visitors and for our plans for paying guests at a later date.

I'd prepared the biggest bedroom for Bob and Peg and it looked very nice and inviting, with its stunning views down over the plain and across to the mountains and volcanic chain.

Because shutters are the norm, as are lace curtains, many French houses, especially older ones, tend not to have curtains as well. I thought the bedrooms upstairs would look even nicer with some curtains and we had plenty to spare, having brought the contents of three houses out to France with us.

I love potching away at what I call BIY – bodge-it-yourself – because I'm not very good at it, so I thought putting up some curtain rails would be something I could possibly manage. But first I needed to go and buy some.

I wasn't entirely sure what they were called in French but I've never been daunted by such minor details. I managed a quick foray to the nearest DIY shop whilst Hippy Chick was seeing to Mother and asked for 'the thing to hold curtains to a window'. I was pointed towards the *tringles à rideaux* and was surprised at how expensive they were, compared to those in the UK.

Then later on, armed with my trusty electric drill, which had known plenty of abuse in my hands, I started drilling holes to attach the rail.

What a good job the French have the very sensible idea of encasing things like main electric cables inside protective trunking, otherwise I would have drilled right through the electricity supply.

As it was, I managed to put up curtains on rails which were very nearly straight, and was ridiculously proud of my efforts.

For some reason which I don't profess to understand, entertaining has always been a bit of a minefield for my brother. In principle, he likes doing it. He's a good cook, an especially good pastry cook, and loves doing elaborate meals. But he also keeps very bizarre hours and expects other people to abide by his rules. It's nothing for him to be in bed by eight o'clock in the evening, nine at the latest, albeit listening to a play on Radio 4. He can't seem to comprehend that that is very far from the norm and most people are up much later than that and probably only just contemplating their evening meal, never mind heading to bed by that time. Especially in France, where the evening meal is often eaten later than is usual in the UK and even young children tend to be up quite late.

We'd supplied detailed instructions to Bob and Peg on how to find the Pink House but, being them, they got lost several times and were late and arrived all of a flurry. But they kindly arrived laden down with gifts for us, Spanish ceramics for me, wine for my brother (they weren't truly aware of the extent of his problems at this time) and, best of all, Peg had picked out a really pretty little scarf for Mother, all sparkling with scattered sequins, which was perfect for the magpie she had become as she got older.

Peg went to sit with Mother who immediately started to chat away happily to her. Mother had lately started to say some quite remarkable things with no foundation in fact as she got more mentally muddled by the dementia.

"My mother was German, you know," she said confidentially to a bewildered Peg, who knew that she wasn't. I suppose Mother must have been getting confused with her late mother-in-law who, although she was from Luxembourg, always had an accent which sounded strongly Germanic.

"At the moment she's on an island off the coast of Scotland, looking after the children," she continued.

Peg looked across at me. I shrugged. I'd developed some very Gallic habits already. Nope, no idea at all where that came from.

The weather was still amazingly warm and we were able to sit out on the sunny patio, drinking in the view, whilst waiting to eat. Mother pointed out 'Billinge Lump' to Peg, several times over. Then it was time for us all to adjourn to the big table in the kitchen where we were to eat the meal my brother had been preparing. It smelt good, although it was fairly obvious a lot of the wine and cognac that had gone into preparing the chicken had also found its way down his throat and he had that hard-eyed stare which was always a warning of rough seas ahead.

I took mother in first as it always took ages to do the ritual of taking her to the loo, then manoeuvring her wheelchair along the rather narrow corridor and tight turn, to get her installed at the table. I saw to that whilst Bob and Peg went up to their rooms to freshen up after their long journey.

Mother wasn't a big salad eater, she found chewing and digesting lettuce difficult, but I liked to encourage her to have a bit of greenery. There were two bowls of lettuce on the table, which I thought was a good idea, allowing all five of us to help ourselves at the same time, so I started to help Mother and myself to some from the bowl nearest to us.

Volcanoes tend to give advance warning of eruptions by belching a bit of smoke and fire first. My brother didn't. He snatched the bowl from my hands and shouted extremely loudly: "Not that one, it's the other one, that's the leaves I trimmed off."

He slammed it down onto a nearby work surface with such force I was surprised neither the bowl nor the tiles on the work surface broke under the force. Deaf as she was, even mother winced at the volume of his shouting, and Bob and Peg, who had just come into the kitchen, looked decidedly uncomfortable.

It set the tone for the couple of days Bob and Peg stayed with us. We all spent the time walking on eggshells as my brother descended further and further into one of his drink-fuelled black moods.

On the morning of Bob and Peg's departure, my brother didn't even appear for breakfast. But as they were getting into their car to go, he appeared in the doorway of his ground floor apartment looking absolutely dreadful and saying, rather in the manner of a small boy trotting into his parents' bedroom: "I've been being sick all night."

As I waved Bob and Peg on their way, I was hit with a sudden, overwhelming loneliness and a realisation that, once again, I was on my own with an increasingly dotty Mother and a decidedly depressed dipsomaniac brother. Thank goodness for the comforting presence of huggable Meic, my adored dog.

One of mother's favourite sayings, to which we were treated many times each day, was the old wartime telegram home from a disgruntled soldier who wanted to be bought out of his service contract: "Dear mother, it's a bugger, sell the pig and buy me out."

It fairly well summed up my feelings at watching our guests depart.

Unfortunately I knew what the mother's reply was, and as I'd well and truly burned all my boats in making the move, it applied doubly to me.

"Dear son, pig gone, soldier on."

Chapter Three
House Calls

Better healthcare was one of the reasons my brother and I had moved Mother over to France. So now it was time to get her entered into the system and find out if it really was as good as its reputation, which puts it as one of the best in Europe.

In early 2007, it was still relatively simple for a retired person to get onto the social security system in France. Armed with the right form from the Department of Work and Pensions in the UK, all one had to do was trot along to the nearest *Caisse Primaire d'Assurance Maladie*, or health insurance office, hand over said form, fill out several others, supply a passport photo and be issued with the precious *Carte Vitale*. This is the magic card which enables one to claim social security payment for things like doctors' appointments, prescription charges and hospital visits.

French bureaucracy is legendary. Even the French admit how complex it can be. As I was to discover when it was my turn to log into the system, much depended on which particular pigeon-hole you fitted into in terms of employment status, and that depended largely on what your job was. It seemed my occupation of freelance copywriter was as little known in France as in UK.

But first to get Mother sorted out. My brother was busily to-ing and fro-ing between the Pink House and the crumbling pile in Wales, which had been his home for more than thirty years and which had yet to be sold, so it fell to me to sort everything out for Mother. And because I couldn't leave her, it always involved the almost military exercise of taking her with me.

With help from Hippy Chick, we had got Mother toddling about with her walking frame in the house, but there was no way she could manage stairs, or trundling up and down the steep slope at the back of the house which led from ground level at the front to lower ground level at the side where my van was parked. So I either had to push her in her wheelchair down the slope, which she wasn't keen on, and then back up it, which I was even less keen on, or drive my trusty blue Vauxhall Combo van – Blue by name – up the slope to collect her.

That was all very well when it was dry, but as I discovered to my cost one day, returning from the shops with Mother in the passenger seat, it was perilous after even the slightest bit of rain. We managed the first few metres fine, then Blue would go no further. The more I tried, the more the wheels spun round and the more we slid backwards and sideways until we were wedged against the hedge. Wedged by the passenger door, too, so there was no way at all of extricating Mother and seemingly no way of moving either up or down. The only solution was to keep on sliding back down, being thankful that Mother was too deaf to hear the hideous squealing noises the branches made as they gouged scratches all along the paintwork on the side.

Mother had never been a driver. Her one and only attempt behind the wheel had been when my father decided to let her try putting our old Austin Seven, Gertie, into the garage. Unfortunately he was no teacher by nature and his instructions were not very clear and resulted in Gertie hurtling into the garage, with mother wrestling the wheel, then ploughing straight on through the closed rear doors.

It was probably not fair to use Gertie as a training vehicle anyway, since if ever a car was possessed, it was that one. There was one memorable occasion driving down a steep, cobbled hill in Stockport, when we had been overtaken by one of the rear wheels which had somehow come off and was bounding down the hill in something like a scene from old comic films such as The Keystone Cops.

More memorably was the time we were driving over a level crossing when my father went to change gear and the gear lever came off in his hand.

Mother had never made a second attempt at driving. Her experience had made her a rather nervous passenger, understandably. So I did my best to reassure her that wedging the van into a juniper hedge and sliding backwards, ripping off branches as we went, was exactly what I'd had in mind to finish a shopping trip. I'm not sure she was totally convinced by my explanation of extreme gardening though, as all the way back down the slope she kept making a frightened little ah-ah-ah noise. Fairly similar to the grunting ah-ah-ah's from me which followed as I shoved and hauled her and her wheelchair back up the slope, now rendered perilously slippery underfoot by the rain and by the skid marks left by my efforts to extricate Blue from the mud.

So I was extremely thankful that the day I picked to take Mother to go and do battle with French bureaucracy to get her *Carte Vitale* was bright, warm and sunny. I didn't think I could cope with adverse weather and French officialdom on the same day.

The myth of many expats that all French speak some English may be true in some areas but certainly not in rural parts of the Auvergne. But that in itself was a blessing, as taking Mother out was always a bit tricky, as age and dementia had robbed her of all inhibitions when it came to remarking on people.

I'd got used to her pointing and saying: "Look at that big fatty. What a big bum", and was only thankful the bureaucrats I had to take her to see probably didn't understand a word of her running commentaries like: "Well, she's a dozy cluck, what is she doing? Why is she keeping us waiting all this time? It's ridiculous. It wasn't like that when I worked in the post office in Cambridge Road."

I was hearing a lot more about the Cambridge Road post office of late, although mother hadn't worked there since the 1930s. But her dementia was causing her to regress. She'd always been a very good sleeper, happy to go to bed early and sleep for hours. Lately she had taken to waking up in the wee small hours. I would go into her room, having heard her trying to get out of bed and ask what she was doing. She would look at me as if I was the one whose mind was going and say: "I'm going to work, of course, at Cambridge Road post office."

Taking her into shops was just like taking a fidgety small child. As her sense of time had completely deserted her, after a matter of only a few moments, she would start doing huge theatrical sighs, and saying to me in an extremely loud voice: "Aren't they dozy in here? Why don't they get a move on?"

So I was heartily relieved to find a kind, sympathetic and efficient woman on the desk to deal with us. Incredibly, it all went like clockwork. I produced Mother's birth certificate, in English, and it was accepted without a murmur. When it was later time to sort out my own *carte vitale* from a different *caisse*, the dreaded RSI or *Régime Social des Independants*, for the self-employed, not only would they not accept a birth certificate in English, they would only accept a translation from an official court-appointed translator, which was of course not cheap.

But it was no time at all before we had Mother's precious card and could start to try out the French health system. The first step was to select a doctor. One of the things high on my 'to do' list was to get a full review of all the medication Mother was on, as it seemed a colossal amount and included anti-depressants. I was sure she was no longer going to need those with her new lifestyle. There were also morphine patches for the pain of her osteoporosis, which again I thought might be managed a little less drastically now we had her mobile again.

The morphine patches caused her to be sick sometimes and to get very confused, more so than usual. If she saw me peeping round her bedroom door to check on her, she would start calling me either Ethel or Doris, the names of her older and younger sisters.

So I was quite glad to be able to stop the morphine patches and manage her pain levels with simple paracetamol and some gentle exercise. Every morning and evening when the carers came to get her up and put her to bed, we had her walking from her chair in front of the television to her bedroom, usually with her singing the 'Bridal Chorus' from 'Lohengrin' or her other favourite, 'Come Lasses and Lads', or more precisely just la-la-ing along to the tune as she couldn't remember all the words.

Our local mayor's wife had been quite helpful in supplying a list of useful telephone numbers for doctor, vet, chimney sweep and other essential services.

I wasn't sure if she was just pulling my leg when she assured me, in all seriousness, that I must never do any washing on February the nineteenth or we would have adders on our property. It may just be coincidence that I never took any notice of that and we did have adders, and the slightly nastier aspic vipers, at the Pink House.

But then I later discovered many of her recommendations were not up to much, and most of the numbers she gave us were no longer in service. So perhaps that was just her attempt at humour, or perhaps she, as a townie who had moved into a rural area, had fallen for a country person's joke at her expense.

As I didn't know any better, I decided to try the doctor she had suggested, who was in the next town. I had heard French doctors, amazingly, still routinely made house-calls, even for non-emergencies, unlike many of their counterparts in the UK, and thought this would be very useful on occasion, because of the difficulties of getting Mother out and about.

One of my first sorties with Mother in the wheelchair had given me a bit of an anxious moment. I wanted to take her to a little craft fair in the small festival hall of our local *mairie* or town hall. When we arrived, I discovered the only entrance appeared to be up a short flight of stone steps, impossible for me to negotiate with Mother and wheelchair.

Being used to the legally-enforced wheelchair access at all public buildings in UK, I popped my head round the door and asked a lady where the wheelchair ramp was. She said there wasn't one, but to just give her a minute. She then appeared with a small army of helpers, many of them elderly ladies who didn't look a lot younger than Mother.

They trotted down the steps, everybody seized a bit of the chair and Mother was hoisted up, swaying regally and somewhat precariously, as though in a sedan chair, and carried up the steps. It may have been an affront to a disabled person's dignity, but Mother thought it was great fun. She sat la-la-ing away to 'Lohengrin' and conducting imperiously with her arms. She was treated to a repeat performance on the way out. I think it made her day.

I phoned the doctor and was somewhat surprised to speak to her directly, not a receptionist. I explained I needed a medication review for my, by then, ninety-year-old mother, and asked when I could get an appointment for her. Imagine my surprise when she said she would call round once morning surgery was finished the very same day.

The doctor was prompt, efficient and courteous, if a little brusque. She made no effort at all to speak English, not even to Mother, which was perfectly fine. I was able to explain everything and understand her responses, and to tell Mother what was going on.

She gave Mother a thorough examination, including taking her blood pressure, always a tricky manoeuvre. Mother had never had a particularly high pain threshold. How she managed to give birth to two children is a bit of a mystery. I think it's significant that, having given birth to my brother in a hospital, an ordinary one, whatever they were called before the National Health Service was created, two months after his birth, she opted for a private nursing home in which to give birth to me four years later.

Latterly she had become very bad about having her blood pressure taken – she did not like the feel of the cuff tightening on her arm and would let out a constant "ow-ow-ow-ow" all the time until it was deflated.

I had a moment's panic, being slightly dyscalculic and totally rubbish with figures in any language, when the doctor announced Mother's blood pressure was twelve/seven. Then, even my mathematically challenged brain realised that, for some reason French doctors didn't count the zeroes at the end, so with a BP of one twenty over seventy, Mother was much healthier than many people half her age.

We discussed her vast array of medication and the doctor agreed there was enough there for a whole team of old ladies, not just one, and found a few which could safely be withdrawn, including the anti-depressants. The doctor left in place the essentials, like heart and stroke prevention medication, plus calcium with vitamin D, and pain relief, for the osteoporosis. It made a much slimmed down medication list, which was certainly going to make it easier to get them all into Mother morning and evening.

First impressions of French medical system in action? Definitely positive, no complaints there. However this doctor was not to remain Mother's doctor for very long. Surprisingly, for a professional person, she was to become the first and mercifully, to date, the only person, to show any resentment towards 'British who come over here taking advantage of our medical services.'

I would have considered her viewpoint unprofessional in the extreme if she had expressed it to me. But she made the grave error of mentioning it to someone else and that indiscretion resulted very quickly in her ceasing to be the *médecin traitant* (doctor with whom we were registered) for any of us.

Chapter Four
R&R

I've always been a big fan of M*A*S*H; the television series from the seventies and early eighties, not the film. I found they all mumbled so much in the film I couldn't follow what they were saying. The series was about the 4077th MASH, Mobile Army Surgical Hospital, during the Korean War. It starred the sexy Alan Alda – what's not to like? It's where I picked up the phrase R&R, rest and recuperation or rest and relaxation, which is much more a US Army term than a British military one.

It was the one and only television series for which I would take the phone off the hook and refuse all contact with the outside world whilst it was on.

After the first three weeks of looking after Mother full-time, I decided I needed some R&R. Three weeks might not seem a long time but the care was pretty constant, although the carers physically got her out of bed and put her back into it. And of course I had the night shifts, when I would often have to get up several times in the night to go and see why she was unsettled. It was tiring.

Various friends pointed out, no doubt intending to be helpful, that it was just like when they had babies. Except they forgot that they hadn't had their babies in their mid-fifties. Also, as I was to discover at a later stage, I had a serious underlying illness, then undiagnosed, which was contributing to my fatigue. And of course constantly having to walk on eggshells around my brother after the lettuce eruption was taking its toll.

Because the care needed was seven days a week, Hippy Chick couldn't do all of the shifts herself and had brought in more of her staff to cover Mother's needs. The team that was building up was largely a good one. She assured us that if I needed twenty-four-hour cover for the R&R I was planning to award myself once a week, there would be no problem at all, and that the night shift would always be covered by herself or by one of the other older, experienced carers.

One day I opened the door to the carer coming to do the evening shift. She looked about sixteen. She also had the most stunning blue eyes. Most of the girls who came spoke very basic school English and all tried to make an effort with Mother, but they always managed to muddle along between them, despite the language barrier.

I usually tried to pop out with Meic, my dog, in the half hour the carers were there in the evenings, as otherwise I was a bit marooned at the house. Luckily, at thirteen years old and with a weak heart, he didn't need a lot of exercise, but we were both always glad of a breath of fresh air, after being cooped up in the house all day on Mother-sitting duty.

The newest young carer told us her name was Aurelie but suggested that might be a bit difficult for Mother to manage and remember, so suggested we call her Lili. She made an instant connection with Mother, who immediately started kissing her hands and telling her she loved her.

I was never sure if these expressions of love and affection to the carers were within Mother's control, designed to make me jealous, or just another manifestation of the dementia. I certainly never got anything similar. In fact I was public enemy number one.

"Here's your tea, Mother."

"Too hot/too cold, too sweet/not sweet enough," according to her mood of the day. It seemed whatever I did was not right. I managed not to take it personally, as I'd heard many other carers and relatives of elderly parents with dementia say it was always the closest family who were under attack.

It used to remind me of the lines from Dylan Thomas's 'Under Milk Wood', the exchange between Mr and Mrs Pugh, along the lines of: "Here's your arsenic dear, and your weed-killer biscuit. ... Here's your nice tea, dear."

"Too much sugar."

"You haven't tasted it yet dear."

"Too much milk, then."

I'd always quoted the first line to Mother whenever I handed her a cup of tea, and luckily she always remembered where it came from. I said it a few times to her in the nursing home in Wales and got some very strange looks. Obviously literature was not the favourite subject of many of the staff and they were unaware of Dylan Thomas, despite the fact that those very words had been penned not many miles from the home, at The Boathouse, in Laugharne,

Mother was never very good at languages, although she had picked up a few words of French on her trips to her in-laws in Luxembourg, of which her favourite was definitely *fatiguée*. She was happily telling Lili she was *fatiguée* and Lili was telling her, in her delightful English: "We go to bed now, darlink," so I knew it was safe to leave them to it while I took Meic out.

I was even more relieved, when I passed Lili's car, to see a toddler seat in the back. Although Lili looked very young, if she had a baby, that more than equipped her for caring for Mother's needs, in my book. I was later to discover Lili was older than she looked, in her mid twenties.

So I set about preparing my first twenty-four hour R&R. I'm a compulsive list maker. I make lists for everything, from shopping trips to holidays. The first thing on many of my lists is often: 1. Make a list.

I made long careful lists to cover everything which might arise during the whole of my twenty-four hour absence, what meals I'd left for mother, what TV channels she liked to watch and when, and what medication she needed at what time.

I started looking at maps and local guide books to decide where Meic and I were going to go on our little adventure. I didn't plan on going far, just in case for any reason I was called back for an emergency. I planned to find the nearest local campsite I could, and some nice leisurely walks round and about that would suit Meic's restricted exercise needs.

I was going to leave at two o'clock on a Monday afternoon and be back for two o'clock on the Tuesday. Hippy Chick was covering the night shift and the morning of my return, one of the other girls would cover the afternoon of my departure. My brother would, of course, be there the whole time but he neither suggested he should cover some of the hours himself, to save on cost, nor would I have proposed it. He had always refused point blank to do the tricky things like take Mother to the loo, and had little patience with helping her to eat or giving her her medication.

From looking at books of the area, and doing some Internet research, I'd settled on spending the afternoon at Le Gour de Tazenat, a volcanic lake just a ten minute drive from the Pink House, followed by camping at the nearby town of Châtel-Guyon.

The lake was the northern-most point of the volcanic chain running through the Puy de Dome *département*, and according to the local guide book, was to be found in the small commune of Coal Scuttle the Old Ladies. Yes, I kid you not. It's never, ever a good idea to try to translate place names into English, along with the rest of your web page, but that is what can happen if you allow an automatic online translator to do its worst. Charbonnières-les-Vieilles is a perfectly acceptable name for a commune and certainly makes a lot more sense than Coal Scuttle the Old Ladies.

As soon as Lili had arrived I settled both her and Mother in front of 'Escape to the Country' on the television. The carers became big fans of British TV through those times of sitting with Mother; Lili even stayed on longer on one R&R cover just to find out how the kidnap of Dr Jimmy panned out on Doctors. Then Meic and I jumped into trusty Blue, the Combo van, and trundled off up the road, feeling like a pair of naughty school children bunking off from double maths.

Yes, I know. Even if dogs have feelings, I couldn't possibly know what Meic's were. That's how I felt. If border collies are capable of feeling any such emotion, Meic was probably feeling excited anticipation of a walk in a different area at the end of a car journey, both of which he loved.

We were very soon at the little track which led to the lake, so Meic and I set off on our planned gentle stroll in the pleasant spring sunshine. This was my first experience of following French signposts for footpaths. I should have remembered, in picking the yellow butterfly marker which said it marked an easy route, suitable for families, that this was the nation which trained the formidable Foreign Legion.

I probably missed a marker somewhere on the way, assuming that the route would probably keep close to the edge of the lake, but Meic and I soon found ourselves scrambling up and down steep wooden steps cut into the side of hills and gullies, and picking our way precariously over slippery tree roots rather too close for comfort to the water's edge.

I was a bit concerned about Meic's heart condition and kept stopping for a little breather, but he was clearly having a brilliant time and was doing much better than I was, lumbering up the slopes. I walked him on a harness and lead and a few times was pleased to have his help on the steeper bits.

The afternoon was becoming very warm and as we rounded another bend in our nearly non-existent trail, we were confronted with a stiff climb up some rocks. Intrepid Meic led the way, totally oblivious to my attempts to get him to slow down and remember he was supposed to have died from heart failure three years ago.

We made it to the top without incident, paused for a very welcome shared drink from my water bottle, then enjoyed the ease of a downhill slope all the way back to the van, and then the leisurely drive, not very far, to the campsite I had chosen .

It was more urban than I had hoped, with traffic noise nearby, but it would do us for the night and we were the only tenting campers there, so no one to disturb us. I quickly pitched our tent, got out the little Twister camping stove to make some supper, and settled down to enjoy a leisurely meal, listening to birdsong, and without the need to attend to feeding Mother.

I was delighted when, later that evening, a nightingale started up its beautiful fluting melody, showing off its full and very impressive repertoire. I was considerably less delighted when, by five the next morning, it was still singing away lustily and I was still wide awake.

After a leisurely breakfast for us both, a very much half-asleep one for me, I drove us slowly back across country to the Pink House, stopping off a couple of times on the way for little walks and cups of tea, whilst drinking in the views.

Meic was as much of a tea addict as I am. Whenever I brewed up for me, I always made him a little bowlful of tea, which he thoroughly enjoyed. He even seemed to share my taste for the very weak and highly fragrant blends the French are so fond of, my favourites being Russian

Earl Grey and Russian Lady Grey, both served up in a way to make the purists shudder - with milk, and honey.

I was determined to be back at the Pink House on the dot of two o'clock to take over from Hippy Chick, so as not to give my brother chance to raise objections to future R&Rs as, despite the lack of sleep, I had so enjoyed my little break. I'd lived alone for more than twenty years at this point in my life and was finding it very hard to adjust to sharing a house, albeit one as big as the Pink House, with its three storeys and seven bedrooms, with Mother, Brother, and a procession of carers. As I pulled into the driveway, I noticed that Hippy Chick's car was not there, but my brother's motorhome, the Dingley, was. I assumed that my brother had let Hippy Chick go a few moments early, knowing I would be back on time. The sliding garage door was shut, so I couldn't put Blue away, but as I wanted to air all my camping gear before packing it away, I parked Blue outside the garage door and went up the steps to the front door, which was locked.

Getting a bit concerned by now, I got my keys out and let myself in. No signs anywhere of Hippy Chick, my mother or my brother. The house was quiet and empty, no trace of anyone, no note anywhere. Slightly more worryingly, the folding ambulance chair my brother used sometimes for manoeuvring mother to and fro when we took her out together in the Dingley, was at the bottom of the garden steps, suggesting she had been taken out somewhere, hopefully not for any medical emergency reasons.

I tried calling and texting my brother's mobile with no result; it simply went straight to voicemail. And I realised I, rather foolishly, didn't have Hippy Chick's mobile number, so there was nothing else Meic and I could do but sit and wait.

About forty-five minutes later, Hippy Chick's car pulled into the driveway, so I hurried down the steps to find out what had been going on. Hippy Chick was driving, and smiling, Mother was in the front passenger seat, smiling, looking pink-cheeked and very happy. My brother was in the rear seat, looking very much the worse for wear and scowling furiously.

Hippy Chick explained that they had taken Mother out to lunch and all had a very good time. My brother said there had clearly been something wrong with the food as it had made him ill. It was obvious to everyone it was not the food which had made him ill. He announced that he was going straight to his apartment to be sick and/or lie down, in no particular order.

This left Hippy Chick and me to haul Mother up the steps in the ambulance chair and install her in front of the television for the afternoon. Hippy Chick explained that although Mother had had a very nice time and eaten well, my brother had mainly concentrated on drinking, both wine and spirits.

He didn't reappear again at all until the following morning, so it was straight back to just me and Mother. It was almost as if that was my pay-off for time away, although that was what we had agreed. Back down to earth with a bump after my first R&R.

Chapter Five
Testing Healthcare

The first few weeks in France had been idyllic, with Mother improving every day and my brother much calmer and, seemingly, drinking less. But if the catalyst of having visitors had prompted the explosion over the lettuce, my R&R days seemed to be like a red rag to a bull.

Whilst agreeing that they were essential for me, and were great for mother, as Hippy Chick always took her out somewhere nice and made a big fuss of her, my brother seemed to be consumed with jealousy by my little trips. Or perhaps by my self-sufficiency and spirit of adventure, which he clearly envied but didn't entirely share.

His idea of a nice break was an hotel, with food and drink. As long as I was with my beloved dog, Meic, I didn't mind if we finished up sleeping in the back of the van in the middle of nowhere, which we did on more than one occasion when we couldn't find a suitable campsite.

I never quite knew what sort of a reception I would get when I arrived back. Invariably my brother would have been drinking heavily, as with Hippy Chick doing the driving and looking after Mother, there was no need for him to refrain from drinking when they took Mother out.

As well as a list-making fanatic, I'm also a compulsive planner, who gets probably as much enjoyment from planning trips as actually going on them. Often, as Meic and I sat outside the tent in the sunshine on one R&R day, I'd have the maps and guide books out and already be planning our next adventure.

I'd pick an area from the guide book based on an interesting walk, or bird sighting, or other wildlife feature, then look for a nearby campsite. If there wasn't one, Meic and I curled up in the back of the van quite comfortably.

Sometimes I didn't go very far, if I was more concerned than usual with how my brother was behaving and was anxious not to be too far away in case I got called back. The Gour de Tazenat became a favourite place to go and camp out in the van as it was very quiet and I had now found the way to drive round and park up high above the rocks Meic and I had scrambled up. We'd also found the proper circular walk round the lake which was far less strenuous than the one we had done.

After a nice walk, a campfire supper and relaxing either with maps or a book, Meic and I would climb into the back of the van, unroll my sleeping mat and Meic's dog bed, hang towels and travel rugs at each window and snuggle down for the night.

One night I was just drifting peacefully off to sleep when I felt the van begin to rock and sway gently. My first thought, as ever, was that Meic was starting one of his psycho-motor seizures, a type of epilepsy. Reaching out a sleepy hand, though, I could feel that he was happily stretched out quietly and breathing deeply.

The next thought was high winds, as the weather could blow up very quickly on the Massif Central, one minute quiet and calm, the next blowing a hooley. But there was no sound of any wind. The night was still, cold and twinkling with bright starlight.

I knelt up and carefully peeped out from under the blanket covering the back windows, a little fearful of what might be lurking outside, since there was not a soul around, or should not have been. By the bright moonlight, I could see a large wild boar, calmly scratching himself against the back of the van. I just hoped the brake was on sufficiently, and that I had left the van in gear, in case his scratching got any more vigorous and we found ourselves rolling down the very steep rocky slope into the cold volcanic lake below.

Luckily, after a jolly good scratch, the boar trotted off on his way and left us in peace for the rest of the night. It made me extra careful of where I parked the van on future wild camping trips and meant I would often put a large rock to block the wheels, just in case.

I was always very careful to be back on time from my trips, not only because of my brother's reaction but out of fairness to the carers, who often had to be somewhere else, with very little travelling time allowed between clients.

On one occasion, I was cutting it a bit fine, though not intentionally, all because of the dreaded rural French *déviation*. A *déviation* is a diversion, usually for roadworks or something similar, but the rules governing them are a bit different out in the sticks.

The start is always carefully marked, and for the first few road junctions, there are nice clear yellow signs showing you which way to go. Then inevitably, the further off the beaten track you drive, the fewer and further between the signs become until finally, once you have lost all sense of direction and there is not a landmark in sight, the signs disappear altogether.

Probably fine if you have a GPS. I don't. I'm such a technophobe, I couldn't get to grips with the one my brother once very kindly gave me. I couldn't even succeed in mounting it on the dashboard. And I certainly couldn't have coped with putting my trust in a disembodied voice telling me when to turn left, turn right or go straight on. I'm too much of a control freak. So he kept it himself.

I prefer the old fashioned method of maps and compass and can usually get about fine, although I did discover that many of the roads around here had had their numbers changed since my maps were printed. But I managed to get back on time, by the skin of my teeth.

Once again, my brother was in a bad way. Hippy Chick warned me, before she left, that he seemed in a particularly volatile state and wished me *bon courage* for the explosion which was no doubt about to take place.

My brother had bought a couple of maps of the area, before I'd had chance to buy any. My only shopping time was my twenty-four hours R&R, which I generally preferred to spend well away from crowded shops. As I was venturing further afield on that particular occasion, I had borrowed them from the kitchen where they lived. I knew my brother would have had no need for them since he was only going out with Hippy Chick, who knew the local area well, and had a GPS. I should probably have asked him, or at least told him I was taking them, to be sure of being back on time.

Ballistic accurately sums up his greeting to me. He shouted and raged, accused me of 'stealing' the maps and threatened to call the police. I told him to go ahead. I encouraged him to. I begged him to. I thought perhaps the sight of uniformed and usually armed *gendarmes* arriving to investigate the 'theft' of maps which I had borrowed for twenty-four hours and returned in their original condition might bring him to his senses a little.

He continued to rant, but when I pointed out that he had no need of them as he was with Hippy Chick, he calmed down a little, agreed that was a fair point, and stumped off back to his apartment to 'sleep it off'.

It was to be another of his recent behaviour patterns, disappearing into his flat for days at a time, armed with bottles and boxes of wine and not reappearing even to eat. And, when he did finally surface, looking truly awful.

After one such session he looked so bad I called the doctor, who immediately arranged for him to be taken to the nearest hospital by ambulance.

I quickly found one of the huge benefits of the French healthcare system compared to that in the UK. Whenever Mother was admitted to hospital in England, if I phoned up for news, despite being a two-hour drive away, being her next of kin, and holding joint enduring power of attorney for all her affairs, it was almost impossible to get any information about what was going on.

In France I, as next of kin and the person most directly affected, was kept informed every step of the way. The hospital phoned me, since clearly I couldn't leave Mother alone to go there, to say that they had assessed my brother and arranged his transfer to a psychiatric hospital in Clermont-Ferrand, where they felt he could receive the best possible care and help for his depression.

And very shortly after his arrival there, that hospital phoned me to say despite all their best efforts, they had not been able to persuade him to stay and he was consequently on his way back to the Pink House in more or less the same condition in which they received him, just slightly less the worse for alcoholic wear.

Exactly the same thing happened a couple of weeks later; this time he had to be carted off to hospital on a Sunday which effectively put paid to my planned R&R the following day, as yet again, my brother was refusing to stay. The hospital phoned to say I should go in for a care plan meeting with them and try to persuade him to accept some proper help with the depression, which would at the same time help with the drinking.

Hippy Chick had explained that I could, effectively, have my brother committed against his will, to force him to accept proper help for his conditions. But I was very loath to even consider going down that route for two reasons. First, I knew that successful withdrawal from alcohol addiction was very unlikely unless it was the addict themself who took the conscious step to get help. And secondly, I could just imagine the repercussions if I did, bearing in mind I was living in my brother's house, to which I had no legal title.

I didn't see how it would help Mother in any way if I was thrown out into the street and had to leave her there.

So instead of our usual twenty-four hours of blissful freedom together, I had to leave poor old Meic at the house, cancel the overnight cover, and go off to the university hospital in Clermont-Ferrand. Before going in to see my brother, I had a long and amazingly frank discussion with a young doctor in which she told me more than I would have imagined. Then we both went in to the private room in which my brother was.

He already looked considerably better for drying out overnight and had showered and cleaned himself up a bit. I knew he was, as usual, building up to saying he was absolutely fine and ready to go back home.

Backed by the extremely supportive young doctor, I pointed out that he clearly had major problems, and he was obviously not dealing with them by himself. I said that I was not able to do more for him than I had already done, with mother taking up most of my time and attention.

It was real tough love stuff. What the doctor was proposing this time was a longer stay, of two weeks at least, in a private psychiatric clinic with experience of helping people with substance dependency. It would be as a voluntary patient, but with a strongly worded recommendation that this time he agreed to stay there until he was told he was fit for discharge.

My brother was still saying he was absolutely fine, he could manage by himself, he would stop drinking and would remember to take his medication for depression. I pointed out that his problems were not making my or Mother's lives easy or pleasant, and that seeing him in the state he got himself into was extremely upsetting for Mother and not at all what she needed.

Then I played my trump card. I told him I had looked into the procedure required to have him committed, against his will if necessary, and said that, unless he agreed to go willingly, that was exactly what I would do, fervently hoping that he would not call my bluff.

Backed up by the young doctor, who agreed with everything I said, he was forced into a corner and meekly agreed to go to the clinic as a voluntary patient a couple of days later when there was a bed free and the university hospital considered him fit for transfer.

* * *

With my brother safely out of the way and receiving professional help, things were much more relaxed at home and I was able to take Mother out and about for little trips. I took her to the bank to sort out a bank account for her, to the hairdressers, and on several picnics, including up to the Gour de Tazenat. The view from up there was truly spectacular, looking across the lake to the distant Puy de Dôme and its flanking chain of lesser volcanoes. As soon as I got Mother and her chair out of the van for a breath of fresh air, she looked across at the Puy and asked: "Is that Billinge Lump?"

The French have a reputation for being rude. It's probably true in the big cities but certainly not in rural Auvergne, where we were always greeted politely wherever we went.

The traditional greeting on entering a shop or similar, if there are customers of both sexes waiting, is simply to say: *Messieurs, 'dames* (gentlemen, ladies). All right, perhaps French greetings are a bit sexist, but still polite.

Madame, or the plural *mesdames*, is often abbreviated for ease, so sometimes the greeting is just *dames* if there are only ladies present, which is, of course, pronounced like the English word damn.

One day as I pushed Mother's wheelchair down the main street of our little local town on the way to the hairdresser, a couple of women were standing talking on the pavement, effectively blocking it. They immediately stepped aside into the road and politely greeted us with '*dames*' as we passed them.

Unfortunately Mother had new batteries in her hearing aid so caught the word and took it for 'damn'. I had to scuttle her at speed off up the road as she began a tirade of: "Well, that was rude, why did they swear at us just because we wanted to go past?"

I also learned that day about making snap judgements. I try not to be judgemental but sometimes it is easy to look at something or someone and see something completely different to what is actually there.

After Mother's hairdo, I took her back to the van, opened the driver's door, threw my bag onto my seat, then took Mother round to the passenger door to transfer her to the seat and put the wheelchair in the back of the van.

I became aware of a young man standing not very far away. He was very thin and pale, and despite my best intentions, my immediate thought was 'crackhead', especially with the way he seemed to be eyeing up my bag, which was beyond my easy grabbing range.

I was so wrong. As soon as I started to heft Mother out of the chair and transfer her to the van, no easy task, despite her small size, he called across to ask if I needed a *'coup de main'*, if he could give me a hand.

My brother had now been in the clinic for five days, which was a record. He was in contact with me frequently. On the first few days I got great long lachrymose texts full of apology for how he had been behaving and the problems it had caused for me and the upset caused to Mother.

He was of course starting to dry out and is often the case with him, once he starts to feel a bit better, one of the first things he wants to do is polish up his shoes, a hangover from his naval service days. Unsurprisingly, boot polish was not something provided by even the impressive French healthcare system.

I agreed to get cover for Mother for a few hours at the weekend and drove down with his post and a few essential items, like decent strength teabags, which are very hard to come by in many parts of France, and shoe polish. I took Meic with me for a little run out.

My brother appeared quite well. We sat outside in the grounds of the clinic and used my little camping stove to brew up cups of tea to go with the cake and biscuits I'd brought. My brother spoke of how much better he was feeling, how much progress he was making and how he hoped to be back in another week or so, feeling he had his life very much back on track.

Ever the optimist, I hoped this might well be the new beginning I had hoped he would make with the move to France, especially as he promised faithfully that this time he would not leave the clinic until the doctors pronounced him fit to do so, and this was a first. Previously the longest he had stayed anywhere which might have been able to help him was thirty-six hours.

Whilst he was away, I decided to tackle the appalling state of his apartment, thinking if he did arrive back feeling much better, it would not be helpful to have to return to the state of squalor in which he had been living.

Any living space he occupied was always reduced to a slum within a very short time. This had always been the case, throughout much of his life. It was why he had opted to occupy the very small downstairs flat rather than the spacious top floor apartment of the Pink House, thinking that in a small space, he may be less inclined to spread his possessions around too much. Wrong!

Knowing he hated having his property touched, a long-established phobia since our father threw away all his personal possessions when he went away to sea, I carefully sorted and stacked everything into boxes, labelling paperwork as best I could. I tried to adopt some sort of logical filing system, based on the time I had worked as a case tracker for the Crown Prosecution Service.

I cleaned and tidied everywhere, remade the bed – the mattress was beyond redemption so I replaced it and got clean new bed linen. Although the apartment was only two rooms and a bathroom, it took me the best part of two days and a half days to get it back under control.

After two weeks in the clinic, my brother announced that he was allowed to go home. He assured me he was feeling much better and calmer, had medication to help him, which he promised faithfully to take. He said he hadn't had a drink in over a fortnight and no longer wanted or needed alcohol, so could I go down and collect him, since he had been taken there by ambulance and he had no means of getting home otherwise.

It meant another R&R compromised but I agreed to go down on the Monday afternoon, call in with various things he wanted, find a campsite in the area and spend the night there, then collect him the following day and take him back to the Pink House.

I found a nearby campsite, which was pleasant enough, and was my first experience of staying on a Dutch owned campsite in France. Any Dutch readers had better look away now, as it was not a very positive experience.

When I went to book and pay, the man on reception, who was admittedly the father of one of the owners, not the owner himself, did not speak a word of French. I always begin by speaking French wherever I go so I was surprised, but then less so as I looked around the campsite for a suitable pitch and found that with the exception of myself and one French family, every single other pitch that was occupied by Dutch people. I was used to being the only Brit on French campsites, but to find myself and the French outnumbered on a site in their own country, was decidedly odd. And the French family certainly seemed pleased to hear a *bonjour* from me, seemingly the first of their stay, as I walked past to find the *sanitaires*, or washing facilities.

As usual, I pitched my tent, set up camp ready for the night, then Meic and I went off in the van to find somewhere to walk.

The French love their religious statues and always seem to build them on the highest and least accessible hills, puys and lumps of rock they could find.

In the distance I could see a white statue which looked like the Virgin Mary, perched on top of a small rocky outcrop, so I headed for that. The drive up was not for the faint-hearted and you certainly needed to be good at hill starts if you were unfortunate enough to meet any other traffic coming down. But the spectacular panoramic view from the top was well worth the effort.

Best of all, as Meic and I wandered peacefully about the deserted site, looking at the huge and beautifully sculpted statue and the old canon which was also placed there, we were literally buzzed by dozens of beautiful swallowtail butterflies. Quite a rare sight in most of the UK, up there they were as abundant as midges and mobbing us in a similar way.

The next morning, we collected a very presentable-looking brother and drove back to the Pink House, where he made a fuss of mother and settled back into his daily routine for a couple of days before taking himself back off to the UK for a Russian summer school in Essex.

So far so good. He seemed like a reformed character. But how long would it last?

Chapter Six
More Visitors

With my brother safely out of the way in the UK for a few weeks, things were very much more relaxed and I could enjoy the next round of visitors. Both Meg, my oldest friend from school days and Jill, my very best friend, were keen to come and see the Pink House for themselves.

Jill had, of course, been to the Auvergne before. She came with me on my first voyage of discovery around the region (described in *Sell the Pig*), and had also done one of her many equestrian holidays in the area, including riding up the Puy de Dôme volcano on a tour of the region. In fact it would be quicker to tell you places Jill has not visited, often on horseback. Meg had never been to the region before so was keen to discover it.

In the strange way things tend to work out, both wanted to come on the same dates which was not going to be possible, since I only had a single passenger seat in my van. They managed to stagger their dates so Jill would arrive on a Thursday, I'd take her back to the airport on the following Thursday, then go back to the airport that same evening to collect Meg coming in on a later flight.

That left me the day to strip and change the bed and tidy the house up a bit, in between the usual round of chores involved in looking after Mother. Simple. What could possibly go wrong?

My brother is of course convinced there is some sort of jinx on our family, and after their first visit, Jill and Meg probably came to the same conclusion.

Jill has travelled all over the world by plane, her late father having been a pilot, and seldom had any problems. She's always been the perfect travelling companion for an air travel hater like me as not only does she know the right things to say to keep me relatively calm on the flight, she also knows all the dodges and things to look out for, which have stood us in good stead on our many adventures together.

We once went to the States together to do a trail ride in the Washakie Wilderness region of the Shoshone National Forest in Wyoming. Getting to the town where we needed to pick up the trail ride normally involved taking a very small plane for a connecting flight from various hub airports. I definitely draw the line at small planes, so instead we opted to fly to Denver, Colorado, pick up a hire care and drive up to Riverton, Wyoming.

Despite a fairly useless trail guide who was far too busy impressing his new wife to bother with looking after his customers, we had an enjoyable ride and learned a few important things. Yes, bears really do shit in the woods. So, as on a wilderness pack trail that is also the only option open to humans, you had to be very careful about which tree you went behind.

Secondly, a piece of very valuable advice from the very warm-hearted lady who cooked all our meals, and produced really excellent food on the most basic of equipment. She was very rotund and extremely jolly and told us: "Honey, never trust a skinny cook."

And I learned a very practical lesson. When you stop for your picnic lunch, no matter how hot it is, it is never a good idea to take your hat off and put it down in the grass beside you. When I put mine back on, I found myself sharing it with the biggest wood ant I have ever seen.

When I travel, I need to arrive at the airport ridiculously early to allow myself time to get as calm as possible and also to take as many sedatives as I can before the ordeal of the flight. On our return to Denver, we had an anxious moment trying to drop off the hire car when we could see the depot from the freeway but could not for the life of us find the entrance.

We then had an amusing time getting ourselves a light lunch in a restaurant near the airport, not being sure which meals we would be getting when on a transatlantic flight. After two weeks in the States we had discovered how enormous the meals were, so I ordered just a starter, a prawn salad. When the waitress arrived with it, I had to ask her who else was joining us for lunch as my starter alone would have made an acceptable main course for two people.

Back at the airport and checking in, I was slipping into the comfortable auto-pilot state induced by rather more than the recommended maximum dose of Valium. But eagle-eyed Jill had spotted underhand goings-on with our luggage. It seemed the airline were attempting to bump us to the next flight owing to an overbooking to accommodate several youth football teams heading to the UK for some sort of international tournament.

Now Jill may be a Quaker and so a pacifist by conviction, but it does not do to mess with her. Oh no indeed. As a lecturer in an agriculture college and departmental head of land-based industries, she has a glare which can reduce tough young farm-hands to quivering wrecks if they have the temerity to hand in an assignment past its due date.

In remarkably short order, our luggage was re-labelled and we were back on the flight we had booked. Although sharing with that many young American soccer players was not our idea of a peaceful flight home.

So with all her air travel experience, it was inconceivable that Jill would miss her flight out. But miss it she did, because of a serious accident closing the M4 motorway. There was nothing for it but for her to book into an hotel at the airport for the night and take the first available flight out the next day.

It was great seeing Jill again, and nice for Mother to have some new company, too. She knew Jill, although she always forgot after about five minutes who she was, so I had to introduce her again endless times throughout the day.

There's a joke which goes: one of the good things about dementia is you get to meet lots of new people all the time. Although Mother remembered me, my brother and Meic, anyone else from outside her immediate circle, especially anyone she had met within the past thirty or forty years, was almost always a stranger to her on each new encounter.

We'd take Mother out into the garden to look at the view and she would explain it all to Jill.

"That's Billinge Lump," she'd say to Jill, pointing to the nearest volcano. "We go blackberrying there with my mother. But we have to go early to get the best blackberries, before the thieving pickers get them."

Then pointing to a nearby church, she'd say: "That's Eccleston parish church, where we go to church, and where I teach Sunday School."

And of course poor Jill got this several times a day, so by the end of her stay she probably knew as much about Billinge Lump and the thieving pickers as she did about the Auvergne.

All too soon, it was time to take Jill back to the airport then get the room made up ready for Meg arriving that evening. Back to the airport I went, at ten o'clock that evening, having had a text of confirmation that Meg was on the way. We'd already had the jinx, nothing else could possibly go wrong. Could it?

As there were, at the time, no direct flights from UK into Clermont-Ferrand airport, both Jill and Meg had had to change flights in Paris. Meg was not nearly so widely travelled as Jill and had not previously passed through France's Charles de Gaulle airport, or Roissy as the French rather confusingly call it, so didn't realise quite how large it is. Her UK flight was running slightly late and she was in grave danger of missing her connection to Clermont-Ferrand.

As she had booked through as a connecting flight, Air France were waiting to pounce on her the moment she set foot off her first flight and whisked her, by airport buggy, from one plane to the other, which was literally just on the point of departure.

Unfortunately there was no time to do the same for her luggage in the hold so she arrived in Clermont at ten o'clock at night with just her hand luggage and the clothes she stood up in.

Meg speaks hardly any French so I went to the information desk which was, mercifully, still open at that time of night, although very little else at the airport was. I was already trying to work out in my head how I could fit in another trip to the airport the following day to pick up Meg's luggage. I knew she would be extremely reluctant to borrow my van and do the trip herself, trying to get to grips with driving on the right and coping with the very strange antics of most drivers in the Auvergne.

I was pleasantly surprised when the airport staff assured me that they would deliver the luggage as soon as it arrived on the first available plane. So off I went to take Meg for her first sight of the Pink House and find her at least a spare toothbrush and wash kit, if I could offer nothing else, being of a much smaller clothes size myself.

And deliver they duly did. The next morning, we were still helping Mother to eat her breakfast and take her many tablets, sprays, drops and all the other medication needed to keep her increasingly frail body functioning, when a rather dishy young man arrived at the door with Meg's luggage. We were rather tempted to keep him, but unfortunately, he seemed to be in something of a hurry to escape.

We had three days together at the Pink House, a bit limited by my not being able to leave Mother, but we did the same as with Jill, spent time together in the garden so Mother could tell Meg all about 'Billinge Lump' which she could see from the lawn.

The village the Pink House was in, or to be more precise, on the edge of, had rather a nice quiet little picnic area, just about a kilometre from the house, so while I drove Mother there in the van, Meg strolled down to meet us and we enjoyed a pleasant picnic lunch in the sunshine.

I had actually spent an R&R there, sleeping in the van, when I needed to stay relatively close to the Pink House.

I reminded Mother of another picnic site we had visited together when I lived down in the New Forest and Mother came to visit. If dementia really can be said to have good things about it, one of them is, because of the loss of memory, I could tell Mother the same funny stories over and over again and they would always make her laugh as if it were the first time she had heard them.

Near where I lived in the New Forest lies the brilliant plant nursery, MacPenny's, a fantastic place to find rare and unusual plants. I wanted a schitzostylis for my garden, also known as the kaffir lily, the pretty pink variety called Mrs Hegarty, and knew they would have one, which they did.

Not only do they sell very good plants, they also have the grounds laid out in a series of beautiful woodland walks where you can see plants growing in their natural habitat and get inspiration for your own garden design.

Mother and I wandered about, pointing out to one another interesting and unusual specimens. Then Mother said to me: "Oh look, they've got a picnicaria."

I'm not too bad at botanical names for plants but it was not a Latin name I was familiar with so I was just about to ask Mother which plant that was when I saw the sign she was pointing at: Picnic Area. The story never failed to make her laugh.

Meg was only staying for a long weekend, so I had arranged to take my R&R to coincide with taking her back to the airport and had booked us both a room at the airport hotel so we could see some of the sights, enjoy a nice meal out and, instead of a mad scramble to drive her in to catch her flight in the morning, we could enjoy a leisurely breakfast together. Then she only had to stroll across the quite small parking area, Clermont not boasting a very large airport, and check in for her flight home.

I was now quite happy leaving Mother with the carers, especially when my brother was not there to cause any additional problems for them. The overnight carer was always Hippy Chick herself or one of her more senior helpers, and she assured us this would always be the case. The afternoon and morning slots were usually covered by one of the younger carers, often Lili, our favourite, and they would always be lovely, happy occasions for Mother.

When it was fine and warm enough, the carers would wheel her out into the garden, down the wooden ramp my brother had installed from the sitting room to the patio, to watch the birds and the lizards, or look through Mother's endless collection of photographs, which she always enjoyed.

If the weather wasn't very brilliant, it would be an indoor session, watching English television together. Mother always needed the subtitles on, because she was deaf, so she could follow what was being said much more easily and the girls loved that as it really helped them with their English.

Lili in particular found some of the young presenters on these shows very attractive, but somehow she always managed to fall for the ones who were openly gay and was so disappointed when I told her they were.

The girls were all getting very good at helping mother recite her little poems and sayings, which she liked to do over and over. She loved to say: "Never mind, God is good, and the devil ... not too bad to his own." To which Lili would always chip in with : "Poor devil."

It was all light years from the care Mother had had when living first in her own home then in care and nursing homes in the UK. In France there was none of the constraint on physical contact which has crept into the UK care system. Mother had become very touchy-feely as she got older and dementia took a hold. She loved to take hold of people's hands and kiss them, she loved to have the French kiss on both cheeks from the carers and would often hold onto them a little longer than necessary and kiss them a little longer. It was strange for me to see, as she had never been that way with me, or within the family.

Lili had a little boy, Max, and one evening she asked if she could bring him with her as her childcare arrangements had fallen through. I agreed, thinking it would be nice for mother to have a little one to fuss over.

It amused me to think of how many UK regulations were doubtless being breached as Lili took Max into Mother's bedroom with her and he happily trotted about with her chattering away as she performed intimate toilet procedures on Mother and got her ready for bed. The French generally are so much less prudish than the average Brit about such things and Mother didn't seem to mind in the least. Max came several times to see *la mamie anglaise*, the English granny, as the girls called her.

The girls were also allowed to give Mother her medication, rather than the carers in the UK who were only allowed to put it out for her to take herself, which of course she was incapable of doing. They could help her to eat, if necessary spooning food into her mouth for her when she needed the encouragement, which we were always told they were not allowed to do in the UK. In France it was seen as an essential part of home care, not a case of legal assault.

A single carer, often someone quite small and slight, was not only allowed but expected to transfer Mother from bed, to wheelchair, to armchair, and to lift her in and out of the shower. They were shown how to do it correctly, with no danger to either her or them, and do it they did. Nobody was injured in the process.

It was a huge weight off my mind to know she was being extremely well looked after, fed properly, given her medication, and enjoying a lot of fuss and very affectionate attention whilst I went off for my twenty-four hours to recharge my own batteries.

We'd also applied for and been granted an allowance to pay for some of the cost of Mother's care. She had been assessed as in need of the highest level of care so was entitled to an allocation *personnalisée d'autonomie*, a personal allowance to cover the cost of essential care services for independent living. As Hippy Chick's charges were very high, it didn't cover the entire monthly bill, but it made a good contribution.

So while Meg and I went off on our little jaunt, I knew Mother would be well taken care of and would have a lovely time. I would not be missed in the slightest.

I'd decided to take Meg for a picnic to the hill I'd found with the statue of the blessed virgin on its summit, near to where I had camped when I went to collect my brother from the clinic where he had stayed for two weeks.

It had superb panoramic views of the surrounding countryside and was also a gathering point for clouds of swallow-tail butterflies. They're large and strikingly beautiful butterflies, though with a rather clumsy flight and a somewhat disconcerting habit of flying right at you in an almost menacing fashion.

As we lay in the sunshine, picnicking, reading and snoozing, they were all around and all over us, even landing on us occasionally. Meic was most disgruntled not to be allowed to chase them.

We then headed off, somewhat optimistically, to find a restaurant doing evening meals, me having forgotten that just about everywhere in the entire region is closed on a Monday. In the end we finished up eating at the airport hotel.

Our arrival at the hotel really showed Meg all the things I'd been praising about the area and its low crime rate in particular. The hotel was open, just about everywhere was accessible, but there was not a soul about to greet us, no one on reception, no one in the bar or restaurant, in fact nobody in sight anywhere.

I phoned the number on the card we found, telling us what to do in the absence of anyone on reception, and eventually some cleaning ladies came out and gave us the keys to a room. They told us reception would be manned later that evening. We could easily have had hot showers, a nice snooze and then scarpered without paying our bill.

As is almost always the case, certainly in this region of France, there was absolutely no problem with having Meic in our room or taking him into the bar or restaurant.

We enjoyed our showers, then our evening meal, then a reasonable sleep, although the room was too hot for complete comfort, and then had plenty of time for breakfast before saying our fond farewells.

I arrived back to find Mother, happy and smelling of shampoo, her hair all soft and fluffy, clean and fresh as a small child after bath time, sitting with her carer, both happily engrossed in the latest episode of Doctors, so I barely got a greeting from either of them.

Back in harness and taking up the reins for the six more days before my next R&R – I was really starting to count the days between my little moments of escape.

Chapter Seven
Of Animals and Vets

One of the big differences between me and my brother is our preference for animals. He is cat, always has been, from having a herd of imaginary kittens when he was a small boy, to having a succession of cats through his adult life.

I am dog. For as long as I can remember, I'd wanted a dog of my own, and whilst quite liking cats, if they belonged to someone else, they have never been my first choice of companion.

I got my first dog, a big German Shepherd, when I was nineteen and still living at home. He was a magnificent beast, extremely well bred. According to his impressive pedigree, his name was Velindre Gorsefield Lobo, but he came with the pet name of Perro, Spanish for dog. I finished up shortening his name to something simpler, and actually came up with the diminutive Pez during a Spanish oral exam.

Languages interest me a lot and I'm not too bad at them. Being a reasonable mimic, I can get the accents well enough, and if my grammar is often a little suspect, I manage to muddle my way through and make myself understood. I decided to do Spanish at night school, in case I ever visited the country. I was taking the oral exam and the examiner asked me what I liked to do at the weekends, so I said I went for walks with my dog, *con mi perro*.

He then asked me what my dog's name was: *"¿Cómo se llama su perro?"*

I thought, if I now reply: *"Se llama perro"*, or 'he is called dog', he will probably fail me on my Spanish comprehension. So I came up with the nickname Pez, which stuck thereafter.

My current dog in the move to France, Meic, my big cuddly collie, was my seventh dog and fourth collie. I had brought him to France knowing he was on borrowed time. He was now thirteen and when he was eight, he was diagnosed with a serious heart condition and given an estimated one to two years to live.

We hadn't really given serious thought to a cat for my brother at the Pink House, as he was still dividing his time between there and his house in South Wales which was still unsold. It was in a totally shambolic state and, with the housing market slumping by the day, was proving really difficult to sell, despite now being at an asking price of less than half of its first valuation.

But sometimes, fate has its own ideas on various subjects and we very rapidly went from a zero cat household to a four cat one without even trying.

Whenever Meic and I went on our little R&R camping trips, I always made a point of being back on time. I loved the four years I spent living in Germany where everyone I encountered was very punctual, and where German guests would catch out unwary British hosts by arriving the polite ten minutes before the stated time for social functions, often finding a tardy hostess still in the shower.

I always tried to get back to within a kilometre or so of the Pink House with a good half hour to spare, to allow for unforeseen incidents on the road, and would pass the time giving Meic a short walk and sharing a cup of tea with him.

On one such occasion I had stopped at a picnic site with beautiful views of the surrounding area. It was a pleasantly warm day and Meic and I were strolling aimlessly along a track listening to what I at first took to be the plaintive mewing of one of the many buzzards in the area. But Meic's reaction to the noise quickly made me realise it was not coming from anything feathered.

I let Meic have a longer lead and he was soon snuffling enthusiastically round a small copse of fruit trees whilst the mewing sound got louder.

Looking up I saw, perched in a fork of one of the trees, a pretty young tortoiseshell cat, by this time mewing very insistently to me that she wanted 'Help!' I automatically thought 'she' since somewhere in the recesses of my brain I had a vague notion of having read that tortoiseshell cats are almost always female.

Managing to scramble through the thick undergrowth, I reached up and carefully lifted her out of the tree. She looked to be no more than four months old, was in good condition, with a clean and healthy coat, although she kept insisting she was starving. There were no houses close and she was not wearing a collar, nor could I feel the tell-tale grain of rice sensation of a microchip anywhere about her.

I decided the safest course would be to take her home with me then advertise everywhere locally to say I had found her, in case she was someone's beloved pet and they were distraught at her absence.

Meic, bless him, was quite happy to give up his travel cage for her to travel in and sit in the front passenger well for the short journey back to the Pink House. It was young Lili who was the carer on duty and I asked her if she could help me to bring in a dangerous wild animal I had found and brought home, which was in the travel cage in the van, and needed two people to carry it safely.

Poor Lili looked very apprehensive, not sharing my love of all creatures great and small and being particularly phobic about anything remotely snake-like. So she was heartily relieved to be greeted by nothing more sinister than a loudly meowing small cat.

I took the cat out of the cage and in to see Mother. It was a lovely gentle little cat, very affectionate, and happily accepted being placed on Mother's knee and softly stroked.

Mother always had a way of coming up with names for animals and promptly christened her Mathilda. I found Mathilda some food and water and a makeshift litter tray and she made herself very comfortable indeed, with her paws well and truly under the table.

But no-one warned me of the magnetic effect of having one cat.

Within days, a black cat appeared on the patio and spent a lot of time peering in through the French windows at Mathilda, who spent much of her time in the kitchen. The look seemed to be one of lust, so I assumed the black cat, which I named Blackie – demonstrating that amazing talent which makes me such an original copywriter! - was a male.

Imagine my surprise when, on returning from another R&R trip, Lili informed me that she had seen Blackie disappear behind the old settee I had put under the shade of the overhang so mother could sit comfortably with her legs up. Blackie then reappeared moments later with a little kitten trotting behind her.

I sat quietly and watched and sure enough, first Blackie appeared then an absolutely spitting image of her in miniature. So she was definitely not a male, then.

But there was a bigger surprise to come. Behind the two of them wobbled a little powder puff in beautiful Siamese seal point colours, with a tiny white bindi on her forehead, and with piercing sapphire blue eyes.

The little seal point in particular was so beautiful I decided I simply had to round them up and attempt to tame them. The kittens were about four weeks old and entirely feral, although Blackie was approachable. Blackie and the black kitten were, in fact, not all that difficult to catch and put into Meic's big travel cage. But the other little madam disappeared under very thick rose bushes and I really thought we were never going to get her.

It took me crawling determinedly into the thickest and prickliest part of the bush before she was safely tucked inside my coat, not remotely grateful for being rescued and in fact hissing and spitting with such venom I was heartily glad she was only about four weeks old, and that I was wearing thick leather gardening gloves against the rose thorns.

So mother cat and babies joined the family. I named the kittens Freddie Mercury, the seal point, and Barcelona, the black, despite them both being females, which should give you some idea of my taste in music which is eclectic, to say the least, encompassing Queen, Joan Baez and Kenny Rogers.

My brother, of course, the major cat lover, was delighted to have cats and wouldn't hear of my suggestion of trying to re-home at least some of them. Four females, inevitably, meant some expensive vet bills to get them all sterilised. But we found out that there was a scheme in many rural areas of France with a major feral cat problem, where the local *mairie* and the SPA, the *Société Protectrice des Animaux*, would pay half the cost of neutering strays if anyone adopting them would pay the other half.

A condition of the subsidised scheme was that all cats were tested for FeLV, feline leukaemia virus, a major problem in areas with a high feral cat population. Any which tested positive were put to sleep immediately in an attempt to check the spread of the disease.

Mathilda, or Monster-Mog as I'd taken to calling her because of her bossy and bumptious personality, had clearly been a well-loved pet, but despite all my posters and even placing adverts in the local *Petites Annonces* freesheet, no-one had come forward to claim her. It was quite possible, despite her lack of a microchip to identify her, that she may have had her injections against such diseases. But Blackie, Freddie and Barcie, being feral, stood a big chance of being positive.

Blackie and Monster-Mog were now of an ideal age to be spayed. In fact it was desirable to do Blackie as soon as possible as there was no way we wanted her to be impregnated with another litter of kittens which my brother, no doubt, would also want to keep.

So he took the two of them off to the vet, dropped them off for blood testing, and then called back later that morning for the results of the blood tests. We were both shaken to hear the results – feral Blackie was clear, Mathilda Monster-Mog tested positive for FeLV, so the recommendation was to put her to sleep there and then.

My brother was devastated and couldn't bring himself to give consent. I tried pointing out the practicalities to him, that Mathilda was effectively now a ticking time-bomb who could potentially infect any cat she came into contact with, so would never be able to be let out to wander about and do normal cat things. If we kept all the others vaccinated, she could mix with them but would have to be a house cat for the rest of her life, and there was no guarantee of how long that would be.

He asked them to go ahead and spay her, and he would pay the full cost. So later that day, two still sleepy cats came home, with their sides shaved and stitches in. No more kittens for Blackie and no more freedom for Mathilda.

* * *

Around this time I'd noticed some changes in Meic, my collie. He'd always suffered from psycho-motor seizures, a type of epilepsy, and I'd noticed that the frequency of the fits seemed to be increasing. I'd also noticed he'd started to make a strange noise, somewhere between a cough and a hoarse bark, from time to time, especially if he didn't know whereabouts in the house I was.

Time for a visit to the vets to see what was going on.

I'd always been very lucky with the vets I'd had in UK, and between them they'd managed to diagnose some very rare illnesses amongst the various animals I'd had. If you can call it a distinction, then I had that of owning the first ever horse in the UK, and one of only about seven at the time in Europe, to have equine ehrlichiosis, a type of tick-borne fever.

The vet who diagnosed that, and went on to write a paper about it since it was so rare, became a friend and was a frequent visitor to the riding centre I owned in Wales, bringing his sons there for riding lessons.

A relationship with a vet is a strange one, as it can involve such a range of emotions, from the elation of having a sick animal made better to the devastation of losing a beloved companion. So a vet can see you at your very best and at your very lowest ebb, in tragic circumstances.

I once had to point out gently to that same vet that although I had called him out to put to sleep a pony who was in the end stages of liver disease, it was probably not his best idea to pull the trigger just as I was talking to a potential customer on the cordless telephone, within earshot.

Customer: "What was that noise?"

Me: "Oh nothing, just the vet shooting one of the ponies."

And vets can also see some strange sights in the course of their rounds. Peter, that particular one, told me of his experiences when called to the famous Tipi Valley in Wales, near to where my riding centre was situated.

Tipi Valley was a hippy commune, where the occupants, who legally owned the land they were camped on, opted for an alternative New Age lifestyle. They fought a constant running battle with the local authorities over planning permission to live there. This they dodged by living in tipis, which they would periodically move to a different part of the land so they were not classed as permanent dwellings.

The vet was a bit disgruntled at being called out on the very Saturday afternoon when the Wales v England rugby test match was being shown live on television, in the days long before all this TV on demand stuff. But a goat was in difficulties kidding, so needed his attention.

The valley was inaccessible by vehicle, you had to park some distance away then walk into it, which Peter duly did. There was no-one about, so he figuratively knocked at the nearest tipi and a young woman came out, wearing absolutely nothing but a smile.

A little taken aback, Peter explained that he had come about the goat, so the young woman, much to his relief, said she'd go and put something on then take him to where the goat was.

She reappeared very shortly having put on ... nothing but a pair of welly boots.

So it was off to the vets here in France with Meic, hopefully to forge another long and positive relationship, and get Meic sorted out. I imagined it would probably be something like fluid around his enlarged heart, causing him to cough, and that some water tablets or the like would soon have him right as rain.

It's a sign of advancing age when the first thing that strikes you about a new vet is how young they look. I really did wonder if this one's mother knew that he was out at work. 'Coronation Street' lovers like myself will know exactly what I mean when I say he looked like a very young and very earnest John Stape.

The clinic was fully equipped with absolutely everything needed to perform almost all procedures on site. Some Brits have a strange belief that Britain still holds the monopoly on being a nation of animal lovers and providing the best animal care. My experience with French vets to date has certainly equalled, and in some instances exceeded, the service I received in the UK.

I'd taken Meic in fasting so he could be lightly sedated for X-rays and he happily trotted off with the very nice vet nurse. I went off to do some shopping and came back later for John Stape to tell me the results of the X-rays.

I was totally convinced it was an extension of Meic's heart problems which could be controlled by varying the dose of the Fortekor which was treating his heart failure, successfully, it seemed since he had long outlived the prognosis of Archie, his lovely vet in Market Rasen.

So why was John Stape looking so glum and why did he keep using the word *tumeur* and did it really mean the same as tumour in English? I steeled myself to look at the X-ray he was showing me. It did.

There was more than one tumour, around the trachea, which was what was making Meic's bark sound hoarse. I'm not a vet but even so, I didn't need John Stape to tell me that tumours like those, clustered as they were, would be unlikely to be operable in a young, healthy dog, and certainly not in one of thirteen already suffering from heart failure.

The vet also explained that, given the increase in frequency of Meic's seizures, it was very likely there were secondary tumours elsewhere, possibly on the brain.

Was there any good news? Even just a little crumb? Or were we now at the end of the line?

There was a glimmer. Meic wasn't showing signs of being in any real pain, just a little discomfort, which could be managed with medication – and thankfully he was one of the easiest dogs to medicate I have ever known – and the medication would also, hopefully, retard the rate of growth of the tumours.

So I still had my boy, a little wobbly and sleepy from the sedative, but able to come back to the Pink House with me once more. A few more tents to be pitched together, a few more cups of Russian Earl Grey to share.

* * *

We'd now been living in the Pink House for nearly a year. Mother was blossoming. With help and patience, she could now toddle about the house with her wheeled walker, and I made sure she did walk a bit every day.

It was time for another visit from an old friend. Let's call her Penny. I'd been friendly with her when I'd lived near Market Rasen, drawn together by our love for horses, dogs and all things spiritual. Penny was keen to come but no longer felt confident to drive so far by herself, so I was pleased to find her a co-driver to come with her.

Bob and Peg's oldest son, also called Bob, and always referred to by me as YB, or Young Bobby, was a keen driver. He sometimes did long runs down to Spain to deliver things for a business contact – which makes him sound like a drug or arms runner, but he wasn't.

He'd dropped in a few times at the Pink House on his long runs, for a friendly cuppa and sometimes a bed for the night. He loved driving and travelling and leaped at the chance of the journey.

Penny was a dog owner, like me, but much more pragmatic about hers. When she heard of Meic's latest diagnosis, she suggested it was time to 'give him the lead aspirin' (have him put to sleep) and said perhaps during her visit would be the ideal time to do so, since I would then have the support of friends to get me through a difficult time.

On a practical level she was right, what she said made sense. On another level, I was just not emotionally strong enough to make that decision yet. In a way, Meic was all I had to keep me going. If looking after Mother had ever been a labour of love, it was now more of a daily grind.

Mine had never been an affectionate family. No-one ever said to anyone else "I love you", at least not in my hearing. I still keep a birthday card from Mother to me which simply says: "Best wishes for a happy birthday, love, Mum", with about as much affection as I put in a card to a friend.

And, inevitably, as Mother became more and more dependent on me for everyday things like eating, drinking and going to the loo, I sensed a mounting resentment of me, born out of frustration at her mind and body letting her down.

Meic was my reason to get up in the mornings. He was my go-to guy for a hug when things were hard, a sympathetic ear to listen when I needed to talk. I was not ready to let him go.

Besides, rightly or wrongly, I always stuck by my 'squeaky toy rule'. As long as any dog of mine still had the strength and the desire to play with a favourite squeaky toy, they were not yet ready to make the final journey.

I was thrilled when YB expressed his agreement and understanding when he and Penny arrived. I had recently bought Meic a new squeaky toy, a silly pink hedgehog with an annoyingly high pitched squeak. He loved it. YB and I were watching as he cavorted stiffly and with a bit of a wobble around the lawn, throwing his toy and pouncing on it. YB concurred. It was not yet time to say goodbye.

Penny and YB came over for a few days. We spent the first couple at the Pink House and took Mother on a couple of outings, up to the Gour de Tazenat, so she could point out to them 'Billinge Lump' in the distance, to the big Leclerc supermarket in a nearby town for a super-shop to feed us all for a few days, and a picnic on the way back.

Then the three of us, with Meic, of course, packed up our things for a short trip down to the Sancy Mountains, leaving Mother safely in the hands of her carers.

I had, at this stage, upgraded from my little tent to a camping trailer tent, the sort that unfolded to present a bed raised up off the ground, with a little day sitting area, and a big, roomy awning for dining. My first attempt at pitching it single-handed had been amusing, ending up with me almost managing to shut myself inside the folding bed, like the filling in some giant electric sandwich toaster.

It was ideal for guests as it meant if they were not a couple, one could sleep in the bedroom and the other on a camp bed in the awning, which is what Penny and YB were going to do, while Meic and I shared our little tent.

We had a very jolly evening, all sitting together in the awning, as in true Sancy style, it had started to snow before we'd even got our tents pitched. YB, a guitarist and country singer, had brought along his guitar, so he played and we all sang while Meic kept time with his squeaky toy, mauling and pouncing on it and generally having a brilliant time.

The wine flowed freely, we cooked simple, delicious camp-fire food and sang until we all but lost our voices. And still Meic played on with his squeaky toy.

Then it was time to head our separate ways to bed. I first took Meic along the track to lift his leg before heading for our tent. And then it happened. His legs simply buckled and he collapsed slowly into a heap in the snow. He was still breathing, though with some difficulty.

I ran to get YB to help and between us we carried Meic to my tent and laid him down to make him comfortable. It was the beginning of the end. It was late into the night, the snow was still falling and we'd all been drinking. Even if I'd known where the nearest vet was, it would have been a dangerous and foolhardy journey to attempt to take him there.

As I had done so many times before, I curled up to spoon against his warm body and pulled a blanket over him and my sleeping bag to lie cradling him in my arms all night, hoping against hope he would just relax and let go.

But his big old heart was still beating, although his spirit clearly left him that night in the mountains he loved.

So the following morning, a sad convoy took to the snowy roads, YB driving my van with the trailer tent on the back, as I was in no fit state to drive. Meic lay in the back, still sleeping but clearly now in major heart failure. Penny followed behind in her car.

We arrived at my vets just as they'd shut for the sacrosanct two hour lunch break, which was the minimum anyone took in this area. But John Stape himself answered my urgent ringing of the doorbell. Penny and I carried Meic in then she left me to it.

The vet explained that there was currently no vet nurse on duty and he would normally have one to assist him, but he agreed with me that this deed could not wait another two hours, and I assured him I would be capable of assisting. It would be the last time I could help my boy, and despite the overwhelming sorrow, it was an enormous relief to see him breathe his last slow breath then finally lie at peace.

We drove sadly back to the Pink House. Penny kindly went in first to tell the duty carer the news - it was Lili once again - to make it a little easier for me going in.

Lili, bless her, had grown enormously fond of Meic. She'd always been afraid of big dogs before meeting Meic, who was so gentle, despite his size. She'd become used to taking Mother's empty yoghurt carton to him to be licked clean every morning after breakfast.

More importantly, she knew how much he meant to me, and she and I had become very fond of one another. So she greeted me with a tearful hug which nearly made me lose it altogether.

Amazingly, the first words Mother said to me were: "I'm sorry about Mikey" which, far from comforting me, somehow enraged me. If she was with it enough to have hoisted in and retained what Lili had told her several minutes earlier, what else was she capable of understanding, I wondered, logical thought doubtless warped by grief. Was she just stringing me along some of the time, pretending to be more gaga than she was, for some bizarre agenda of her own?

But of course, I realised she wasn't, it was just that something so poignant had somehow sunk into her befuddled brain and made its mark there.

Just one more day of the comforting presence of friends, then Penny and YB were on their way, leaving me to deal with the abject loneliness of my first dogless days in more than thirty years.

Chapter Eight
Merry Christmas Everyone

Christmas is supposed to be a time of cheer, a time of peace on earth and goodwill to all men, right? Wrong! It's often a time of enormous tension within families and great loneliness for depressed people. It's no coincidence that it's a time of year which sees calls to the Samaritans rise, as well as suicide rates for those who don't make that call or can't get through.

Most of my early childhood memories of Christmas centre around visits from our paternal grandmother. She lived alone, a widow for many years, so often came to stay with us. She was the reigning matriarch of the Luxembourg side of the family or, as we always affectionately called them, the Luxembuggers.

Granny was a consummate linguist, having adequate mastery of six languages, Lëtzebuergesch, or Luxembourgish, her native tongue - and despite what many people think, a High German language in its own right, not merely a dialect - French, German, English, Italian and Esperanto.

Despite her language skills, and despite living in England for more than sixty years, she always retained an accent which sounded strongly Germanic, which caused her some degree of unpleasantness during both World Wars.

It also provided endless entertainment for my brother and me, especially when Granny wanted to clean and ask for the Wim instead of the Vim powder.

Her Vs and Ws were always mixed up, her th's became d's and she always pronounced 'yes' as 'jess'. And she always confused verb structures by incorporating 'to do' where it was not strictly necessary. If she didn't quite catch something we children said, as she was rather deaf, she would always ask Mother: 'Vot does de child say?', which meant my brother and I mumbled deliberately, just to hear her say it.

Her favourite saying of all, which I still use to this day, more than forty years after she died, was always, *'cela va sans dire'* (that goes without saying) as de Frenchman says,' and she always trotted out the entire phrase, as do I still.

One Christmas, my brother and I played a particularly wicked trick on unsuspecting Granny. There were always boxes of chocolates in abundance at Christmas time. One year, as a box was getting particularly low, we carefully unwrapped a beef Oxo cube and put it in an empty space in such a way that Granny was bound to pick it up, and she did. Bizarrely, she didn't seem to mind the taste at all.

Coming up to our first Christmas in the Pink House, my brother was determined to be back in France to spend it with Mother. He'd been spending time in Wales trying desperately to clean up and sell his house there. In the six months I'd spent living there with him, whilst waiting for the purchase of the Pink House to go through, I'd done my best to galvanise him into action to tackle it.

But on his own he simply did not have the strength to face throwing out the thirty years' worth of memories to him, junk to anyone else, he had accumulated. And as long as the house remained crammed with it, it was proving impossible to sell.

He'd arranged to auction it but cried off at the last minute, as even he recognised it was in such a state it was unlikely to attract any bids, certainly nothing like his reserve price.

He'd had a few more episodes of being hospitalised whilst back in Wales, never staying long enough to do any good. He seemed to be having a great deal of difficulty in understanding what I had been going through on getting the news of Meic's terminal illness.

He kept asking what was wrong with me and couldn't seem to accept that knowing my beloved boy was dying was enough to knock me completely off kilter. He kept saying there must be something else. He even got his friend the ex-boxer, who had helped him move the furniture out, to phone me. He, bless him, understood immediately why I was under par, as soon as I told him of Meic's diagnosis.

So when my brother arrived back, obviously keen to find some idyllic family Christmas atmosphere, of which he'd no doubt heard and possibly dreamed but never truly experienced, it filled me with trepidation. That amount of anticipation often leads to extreme disappointment. I should know, I'm an eternal optimist and as such, very prone to feeling let down.

And he should have remembered more about those Christmases of our youth, because what I remembered was discord and tears more than anything else.

My brother and I have always squabbled, as is not unusual in many families. Our legendary Christmas fights over Mars bars became something of a family joke.

I don't remember the full circumstances of it but it seems that one year, my brother and I had each bought the other some Mars bars for a present. I do remember our efforts at hiding them. At one time some were underneath the carpet in the dining room and kept getting walked on till they were squashed beyond recognition.

I also remember every row my brother and I had in the run-up to Christmas always ended with one or other of us shouting: "And you're not getting your Mars bars now, so there!"

There was also the strange ritual of the armchair. This was back in the day when three piece suites were not the norm in every house and there were not the endless furniture sales adverts on television. Ours, and many other houses like it, had assorted armchairs and a divan against the wall, piled with cushions, to take the place of a settee.

One of the Parker Knoll armchairs had wooden arms which were not upholstered. And somehow or another, I always seemed to manage to end Christmas Eve by falling over and banging my head, hard, on one of the wooden arms, and going off to bed with a bump like a duck egg on my head.

There were good times and good memories too, of course, though not as many. Again like many families in those times, our front room, the sitting room, or sometimes just referred to as 'the other room' was reserved for best. On a daily basis we used the kitchen, which had a dining table in it, or the dining room, which also had a table.

The big treat around Christmas time was to go into the 'other room' and crack nuts and eat tangerines. And Mother and I would always read together Dickens' 'A Christmas Carol.' Before I could read sufficiently well, Mother would read it to me. Then as I became more proficient, we would read in turn.

Whenever Mother read to us or told us stories, when she finished she would always say: "The End", with equal weight on both words: "Thee End", then start singing 'da-da-da-da-da' to the tune of 'Come Lasses and Lads'. It's why I chose to end *Sell the Pig* with the words 'The End', when it's not the customary ending to a book.

Christmas in the Auvergne is very much a family occasion. The main Christmas meal, which almost always involves *foie gras*, is usually eaten on Christmas Eve. Boxing Day doesn't exist, either as a day of celebration or as a bank holiday, it's just a normal day.

My brother announced he would be cooking a traditional Christmas lunch. Despite his culinary skills, I did worry about how he would cope with the stress, and decided to have something in which I could give to Mother in case his efforts were not successful.

He wanted an organic capon for the main course. I was apprehensive. Neither Mother's teeth nor her digestive system were what they once were. Lately the only poultry I gave her was cooked long and slowly in stock then liquidised into a type of mush which she could manage.

A great friend of mine, Alex, had been a regular attendee at festivals, where he claimed the only food on offer was always 'pink hippy sloppy' or 'green hippy slop', depending on the colour of the principal vegetable ingredient.

My repertoire of cooking for Mother had become any variation on a theme of pink hippy slop (predominantly carrot), green hippy slop (predominantly broccoli) or yellow hippy slop (predominantly parsnip). I wasn't at all sure how she was going to cope with roast capon, but in the interests of peace on earth and goodwill to all Idiot Brothers, I was willing to bite my tongue.

My brother arrived in the kitchen at about eight o'clock in the morning, long before Mother was up, and began making his preparations. It was clear that he was already well into the Christmas spirit, which was going to be a problem. He was bad enough when drinking copious quantities of wine, but once he started on the hard stuff, he was terrible, and could often become verbally abusive, aggressive and spoiling for a fight.

Accustomed to a gas oven, he had not really got the hang of the electric fan oven in the Pink House kitchen at all, especially with the temperature gauge in Celsius. It was quite a modest sized capon which he was cooking, but he none the less cranked the oven temperature up to hot as the hobs of hell and put it in hours before we would be remotely ready to eat it, given the time it took me to get Mother breakfasted, medicated and toileted in the mornings.

I kept trying to say, as diplomatically as I could, that it was far too early to start cooking, and that, as I was going to be in the kitchen anyway with Mother for at least an hour or so, I'd be more than happy to keep an eye on things and put the bird in at a more suitable time.

The more I tried, the more aggressive my brother became. He kept disappearing off down to his flat and each time he reappeared, he was considerably more drunk than the time before. Then he stopped even trying to hide the fact that he was drinking and came up clutching a bottle of *Pisang Ambon*, the bright green Dutch banana liqueur of which he is particularly fond.

By this time it was getting near the appointed hour for the much vaunted Christmas lunch. I had brought Mother to the table, the capon had taken on all the allure of a very dried-out piece of shoe leather and my brother was clearly heading for another eruption.

I tried as best I could to defuse the situation and deflect the coming explosion, as much to shield Mother as anything else. I suggested my brother go and have a lie down and a long sleep whilst I gave mother some lunch, then he could come back up when he felt more relaxed and have his meal.

He was having none of it. He accused me of all sorts of things, none of them true, then lurched out through the kitchen door, shouting that he was going to go and drink himself to death.

I'm not entirely a heartless cow, although I might well be partly that. But a good friend, who is an alcohol and addiction counsellor, had talked to me at great length and supported me through endless crises and told me exactly how to react in given circumstances. So I said as calmly as I could that if that was what he had decided, then I wasn't going to stop him.

This seemed to totally enrage him as, instead of heading off down the garden steps towards his apartment, he swerved back and lurched right up to the full-length French windows from the kitchen to the patio. Holding the *Pisang Ambon* bottle by the neck, he lifted it up and clubbed it with all his might against the glass.

Thank goodness for double glazing. The outer sheet shattered immediately, sending large pieces of glass flying in all directions. The inner pane cracked, and some shards flew off, but it largely held, mercifully, as Mother was sitting directly opposite it and might otherwise have been showered with glass shrapnel.

Clearly alarmed by what he had done, my brother then quickly turned tail and lurched off down the garden steps as fast as he could without falling over.

Mother was visibly shaken, not fully comprehending what had just happened, and kept asking me in a worried voice: "What did he do that for? Is he all right?"

I tried my best to calm and reassure her. I kept saying he was playing a little joke on us which had gone wrong and not to worry about it.

My first priority was to make absolutely sure there was no broken glass anywhere near Mother, and then to pick up all I could manage of what there was lying about, before any of the cats got themselves cut to ribbons on it.

Next was to make Mother a cup of sweet tea, as much as anything to keep her occupied whilst I phoned Hippy Chick, as I had no idea at all what to do next regarding my brother. As she had two brothers in the *gendarmerie* and a son in training to join, I knew she would know what to do. She advised me to call the *gendarmes* at once, reminding me that in France it is a criminal offence not to help someone in need of it or in danger, and I had no real way of knowing if my brother currently posed a threat to himself, or indeed to me or Mother.

Considering it was Christmas, the *gendarmes* responded quickly to my call, and brought with them a duty doctor. French *gendarmes* are so reassuringly well turned out and polite, I found myself immediately feeling enormously relieved as I explained what had happened and showed them the smashed glass.

Not surprisingly, they asked the obvious question – why was I living there, in the circumstances? They seemed to accept my explanation about looking after my mother, so I took them downstairs to my brother's apartment, never a visit suitable for anyone of a weak disposition, especially after my brother had been in there drinking heavily.

The *gendarmes* went warily in first, picking their shiny-booted way delicately over piles of empty bottles, old newspapers and decaying food, the normal floor-covering in my brother's living space. The doctor followed closely behind, clearly quite shocked by what she was seeing.

The *gendarmes* asked me my brother's name. I always forget the formality of the French and tend to give a first name whereas they prefer a surname, with the formal address of Monsieur. To add to the confusion, my brother's name, Peter, doesn't exist in French, except as the verb to fart.

There was a wretched, curled-up form huddled on the bed, almost hidden beneath layers of filthy bedding. The *gendarmes* stepped gingerly closer, saying politely: "Monsieur Peetaire, Monsieur Peetaire."

My brother opened one bleary eye and looked absolutely delighted to see the visitors. Alcoholics can be highly manipulative. The more intelligent they are, the worse they tend to be. And much of my brother's behaviour is a massive cry for help with his struggle with a world which he simply cannot comprehend, and with which he finds it almost impossible to cope. So to find himself the focus of the undivided attention of two uniformed *gendarmes* and a doctor clearly delighted him.

Despite the huge quantities he had been drinking – I could see from the doorway that the Pisang Ambon bottle was now almost empty – he sat up in bed and said perfectly distinctly: "It's all my sister's fault. She's very cruel to me."

He hadn't seen me, standing as I was behind the doctor and *gendarmes*. He almost certainly would not have said it, had he seen me.

The doctor and *gendarmes* were very kind and considerate. The doctor examined him briefly and announced that he needed to be in hospital. She called the local hospital and arranged an immediate bed for him – yes, in France such things could be done.

These little hospital trips were wonderful for my brother. He really seemed to enjoy them and always kept what he called his 'crash bag' all packed and ready for the next trip.

An ambulance was called, he was loaded onto it, clutching his crash bag and his laptop, which was also packed and ready to go. As they wheeled him out, he saw me and implored me to look after the cats. It was already me who did so, feeding, watering and cleaning up after them.

Then off he went, as happy as anything, leaving me to go back to see to Mother. Luckily, I had a piece of salmon in the fridge for her, suspecting the meal would be a disaster, so I put the dried and shrivelled up capon to one side to cool for the cats and gave Mother a Christmas lunch she enjoyed and could eat, poached salmon, potato purée and steamed vegetables.

I'd also bought one of the delicious ice cream chocolate logs the French do so well as Mother and I both detested heavy fruit puddings in equal measure. After that I could safely park her in front of the Queen's speech whilst I went about trying to disguise the gaping hole and cracks in the French windows, which were directly opposite where Mother always sat at the kitchen table, so she would hopefully forget all about the incident.

Because of her memory loss, she would seldom remember if my brother was about or ask where he was. But she had clearly been rattled by what had happened as, unusually, she asked once or twice that day where he was and if he was all right. She seemed to be perfectly happy with my explanation that he hadn't been feeling well so had gone to lie down.

Later that day I phoned the local hospital for news of my brother, and once again they demonstrated the difference in attitudes between French and English hospitals, telling me everything I, as next of kin, needed to know.

They said my brother was now much calmer and more settled, they were keeping him in overnight to get him stabilised and the next day they would be transferring him to the psychiatric clinic where he had been before. They also told me that his blood alcohol level on admission had been five times the legal driving limit.

It gave Mother and me a few days blessed respite, with him once more safely tucked away in the clinic. But it didn't last long. My brother stayed just a week, before the clinic phoned me to say he was absolutely refusing to stay any longer and threatening to sue them if they tried to make him, so he was on his way back to the Pink House.

He made absolutely no mention of what had occurred, just said they were all idiots at the clinic and it was a waste of his time being there.

He quickly slipped back into his old routine, generally remaining reasonably sober, going out to do the shopping, carting boxes and bottles of wine into his apartment on his return, failing to realise the window of the room I used as an office overlooked where he parked to unload so I could see what was going on.

After a few weeks, he headed off back to Wales, and within a week, he was in hospital there for yet another overnight stay which achieved nothing.

The French have a saying: '*plus ça change, plus c'est la même chose*' (the more it changes, the more it's the same thing).

Ain't that the truth, though?

Chapter Nine
Of Mice and Mules

One of the things some ex-pats complain about long and hard when they arrive in France is their inability to find a doctor/dentist/vet/hairdresser or whatever who speaks English. What a surprise! It genuinely doesn't seem to occur to them that, this being France, most people's first language is French and there is no more reason why they should speak English than an English doctor in Clapham, for example, should speak French.

I was generally managing fairly well with day to day French although of course, inevitably, I dropped some clangers with mixing up words.

One of the carers looked at me as if I was completely mad when I told her proudly one morning that Blackie the cat was a prolific hunter and only that morning had killed a mule and brought it onto the patio to show me.

Except, of course, the word I was looking for was *mulot*, a field mouse, not *mulet*, a mule.

Because of a few old injuries to my neck, starting with a bad whiplash inflicted by a horse throwing up his head just as I was leaning forwards, I was getting a few problems, especially with the amount of lifting I had to do with Mother.

My brother had had a stairlift put in from the lower ground floor, where the garage and his apartment were, to the middle floor on which Mother and I lived. This made it so much easier for me to take her to my van for the little trips out I tried to do with her as often as possible. It meant I was no longer constantly worried about a sudden shower of rain making it impossible for me to drive the van up the slope to the middle level of the house.

But because she was not very steady on her feet, it was far too tricky to let her walk to the top of the stairs to sit on the stairlift in case she fell. So I would wheel her there in her wheelchair then do a dead lift from that to the stairlift chair, and that was taking its toll on my neck.

We had by now changed from the anti-British doctor who thought we were just in France to exploit the health system. She clearly hadn't seen the vast amount of *cotisations*, contributions to the social security system, I was paying, having discovered that part-time workers like me had to pay the same high rate as full-timers.

The change of doctor worked wonderfully well. Although French doctors were quite happy to make house calls, taking Mother to the first doctor's surgery so as not to abuse the system when it was not strictly necessary, had been a bit of an adventure the first time. Fortunately my brother had gone with us, otherwise I would not have managed on my own.

It's still quite commonplace in rural France for doctors to have their surgery in a room of their own house. We set off in good time for an appointment for Mother, having looked up the address of the house in the telephone book.

They're not much into house names or numbers or the like in this area, so we wandered up and down a bit, pushing Mother along in her wheelchair and forlornly looking for some sort of nameplate to give us a clue as to where the surgery was.

We located the house, by process of elimination, but there was still no clue as to which door was the correct entrance to use, and the doors we could find all had steps going up to them so it took both of us to lift the chair up to get in.

The new doctors - there were two of them in the practice, a woman and a man - had a brand new smart, light health centre, with parking directly in front and no steps at all, so really easy access for wheelchairs. The two of them were also young, more dynamic and more open to different ideas and newer methods than our old doctor.

I elected to see the woman, who had already been out to the house to see Mother and seemed very nice and extremely competent. I'd had the neck problems for more than 20 years, so based on previous experience, I was expecting to be fobbed off with anti-inflammatories.

Once, when I lived in Lincolnshire, and was having particular problems, I was sent to the hospital in Lincoln for traction treatment. This involved sitting in a chair whilst wearing something like a scold's bridle contraption, the old medieval public humiliation device for women. Mine had ropes going up over a pulley, with weights hanging off their ends, so my neck was being slowly but constantly stretched, the theory being, presumably, to increase the space between the damaged discs and thus ease the pressure on the trapped nerve which was causing the pain.

All it did was to make me so dizzy that when I drove away afterwards, I managed to bash my VW Golf into a tree I had simply not seen, as a result of which it needed a new door.

The new doctor sensibly decided to send me for my first ever MRI scan to see what was going on before prescribing anything. I was pleasantly surprised at how short the wait was to get one. Not the most comfortable experience I've ever had, as it involved tipping my head back and immobilising it in about the most painful position for my particular injury.

It revealed a ruptured disc, not bad enough to need surgery but enough to make the physio I later consulted exclaim: *"Oh qu'elle est belle!"* (what a beauty), when he looked at the X-rays.

Another difference I encountered when I went back to the doctor to discuss the results of the scan, was that it was a true consultation, in that she didn't just tell me what she was going to do for me. She asked me how I wanted my condition to be managed.

I had already received copies of my scan results both on film, and on disc. In France, everything from blood tests to X-ray results is always sent to the patient as well as the doctor, so one is not left in the dark.

My doctor suggested physiotherapy to ease the problems I was having. She asked if I had heard of micro-physiotherapy, which she felt might be beneficial in my case, and whether or not I would consider it.

The injury itself wasn't major but the combined effects of lifting Mother and spending long hours on the computer doing my copywriting work was making it, literally, a pain in the neck. I had almost constant red hot pins and needles down the back of my neck and into my shoulder and sometimes it became so painful I couldn't even tolerate carrying a very small day rucksack for walks on my R&R days.

I was reminded of one of the old Carry On films where Hattie Jacques, the Matron, was remonstrating with Kenneth Williams, the patient, who was lying on top of the covers on his bed and was, she said, making the ward look untidy.

Williams' riposte, delivered with the acerbity of which he was a master, was along the lines of: if a doctor told him to hang naked from the ceiling by one leg, with his date of birth tattooed on his buttock, he would do it if he felt it could in some way benefit his health. But as he saw no reason why his lying on the bed instead of in it would affect him in any way, he was going to ignore her command.

I was with him on that one. Hanging from the ceiling? Tattooed buttocks? Micro-physiotherapy? Bring it on! Anything that was going to make the pain go away without popping endless pills, was fine by me.

It was considerably easier to get a physiotherapist's appointment in France than I had found in the UK. I simply picked a name from the *pages jaunes* (yellow pages) and found myself being offered an appointment in just two or three weeks time.

It so happened that the appointment date came just three or four days after I had lost my beloved Meic, and it was going to be my first R&R break without him. I simply didn't feel up to going on a trip with my tent without Meic so soon, so I decided to fill my time off with some appointments to sort myself out, physio on the Monday afternoon, the dentist's on the Tuesday morning, and I cancelled the overnight cover and went back to the Pink House to sleep.

The physio I went to see, on the southern edge of Clermont-Ferrand, told me the micro-physio was a very gentle, almost no-touch method of unblocking various energy channels in the body to allow it to heal itself more effectively. She also told me that it could cause great outpourings of emotion, especially after the first treatment, and that if there was no improvement in the condition after three treatments, it was not going to work for my particular condition.

It all sounded a little bit 'woo' to me (a derogatory term used for pseudoscientific explanations) but I was determined to keep an open mind and very determined that I wanted to feel better.

The physio began by asking about my symptoms. When I mentioned the pins and needles in my hands, which I had always assumed were directly linked to the neck problems, she asked me to sit with my elbows on the desk, my arms up and my hands flopped forward from the wrists, then to tell her when and where I felt the pins and needles.

When I did so, she told me the sensation was not coming from my neck and that I had carpal tunnel syndrome. That was a new one on me, I'd never been told that before. But it's not uncommon in people who have suffered wrist injuries and I'd lost track of the number of times I'd sprained one or other wrist in doing crazy things with crazier horses, and during my sixth form years at school when I'd practised judo.

The physio began her stuff. It was all rather strange and a bit mystical and nothing much seemed to be happening. She appeared to make a few passes over my body with her hands, and at one point had hold of one of my feet and had a hand on my head at the same time. But it was not unpleasant, and there was very soothing music playing in the background so I felt very relaxed.

When the session was finished, I thanked the physio politely, made my next appointment for five days' time and left. I'd brought a little picnic with me to make it more of a relaxed outing than just a medical appointment, and I'd noticed a nice park just round the corner, with parking for the van, so I drove there, made my cup of tea, then suddenly started to sob and sob.

I've no idea whether it was the session itself, as the physio had said, the loss of my beloved Meic, or what it was. All I knew was I was sitting in my van absolutely wracked by waves of uncontrollable tears and grief and it went on and on. When finally the tears dried up, I drove back to the Pink House.

The three sessions of micro-physiotherapy did nothing discernible for me, but they had given me the carpal tunnel diagnosis, so my doctor sent me for further tests to confirm it. They consisted of having very fine needles poked into various parts of my hands and wrists and a mild electrical pulse sent down them to check for reactions. Not the most pleasant sensation.

The tests confirmed that it was carpal tunnel and also showed a similar compressing of nerves in the elbows. The sadist, sorry, the doctor who carried out the tests also looked at my rather knobbly knuckles and said I needed to see a rheumatologist as that looked like arthritis.

So another medical appointment, again with hardly any waiting time, and a diagnosis of *rhizarthrose*, degenerative osteoarthritis, affecting principally the joints on my thumbs.

My doctor wrote me a prescription for a chondroitin sulphate capsule and some special supports to wear at night. I duly trotted off to the pharmacy with my prescription.

I'd already found how wonderfully helpful and caring French pharmacists are. The help and advice I'd had from them to date for Mother's medication had been superb. They'd picked up on a few errors in prescribing which the first doctor had made and they were always genuinely interested in our family's health.

Looking at my prescription, the pharmacist asked if I was having problems with arthritis. I intended to tell her I had painful osteoarthritis in my thumbs. Unfortunately, due to a mispronunciation, what I actually said was that my fleas had arthritis. *Pouce* is a thumb, not *puce*, which is a flea, and the vowel sound is subtly, but significantly, different.

It seemed I had to go to Clermont-Ferrand to get one set of wrist supports made to measure, using a substance which was heated until malleable then moulded to the exact shape of my joints.

I was then equipped with a pair of rigid supports, in a fetching electric blue shade, for night-time and a more flexible pair, in black neoprene, for day-time wear. These were equipped with wicked metal blades stitched inside to keep the thumbs supported. If I wore them in public in the UK, I would probably be arrested for carrying offensive weapons.

I affectionately named them my bondage straps and wore them when the pain was bad.

After my latest bloopers with the French language, I decided it might be a good idea to get some help with my grammar and pronunciation. Most of the time I managed quite well, but when I dropped a clanger, it was usually a good 'un.

I'd been really pleased with my efforts to get my UK-registered van re-registered in France and issued with a French number plate. When I have time to prepare for a linguistic challenge, I get the big Collins-Robert dictionary out and plan exactly what I need to say, writing down any new vocabulary I feel I might need, to avoid making too much of a complete twit of myself.

Armed with all the words I felt I would need, I trotted along to the local tax office to get the vital certificate to show I wasn't liable to pay vast amounts of import duty on my old and battered van, so I could then take all my documents to the *sous-préfecture* and get it registered.

I managed to find the right desk, or rather, the little booth, which was apparently the correct place to collect the tax certificate. I launched into my carefully prepared speech, outlining my requirements. But seeing the look of absolute incredulity spreading across the face of the woman attending to me, I began to have a panicky feeling I had instead said something positively obscene or at the very least, asked her to have my baby.

When I faltered to a stop, she stared at me a bit more than said: (in French, of course) "Madame, you are the first English person who has come in here and asked for what they needed in French. They usually just come in and speak English and expect us to understand and to help them."

I rather hoped she was joking. Sadly, I knew she probably wasn't. I apologised on behalf of all lazy ex-pats who made no effort with the language and gained myself more brownie points by pointing out I was only seventy-five per cent British.

On the way back from the tax office, I called in at the shop in town which took adverts for the local free ads weekly and placed two, one offering English lessons in exchange for French, the other proposing an English conversation group.

Being marooned at the house most of the time with Mother, I thought it would be a good way to meet people, to invite them to come to the house. Once Mother was safely in bed of an evening, she was usually quiet for the first few hours so I could safely leave her to sleep while I did my language groups. And if I was at all worried about her, I could use the baby alarm which we had bought so the duty carer, when I was on R&R, could listen in and make sure she was all right.

One of the first ladies to phone up wanted to come in the daytime rather than the evenings, as I had hoped. I explained the problem of having an elderly mother who was slightly gaga. She said she would be delighted to talk to Mother, too. Her own mother had had dementia so she didn't mind in the least.

It worked wonderfully. Gisèle would come on Friday afternoons and take tea and cake with me and Mother. She'd chat to Mother in English, then she and I would converse a bit in French and she'd correct the worst of my mistakes and bad pronunciation.

Another woman also wanted to come during the daytime but she proved to be a very difficult pupil. Her son was a vet, although she insisted on saying veterinarian every time. I tried pointing out to her that that is the American form, in England they are called veterinary surgeons and the abbreviation vet is perfectly acceptable. But no, she stuck with veterinarian. So I was quite pleased when she decided she lived too far away to come again.

One woman phoned me up and said I absolutely must have lessons from her as she was a *parisienne* and only they knew how to speak French correctly. If I let a local teach me, I would finish up with a horrendous Auvergnat accent. Thanks, but no thanks. I quite liked the Auvergnat accent, and I certainly didn't want to stick out like a snobbish sore thumb with a Parisian accent.

I initially got quite a lot of takers for the conversation group. I think about eleven turned up for the first few sessions. It was very challenging, as their wants and abilities were all so vastly different it was really hard to pitch the session to suit them all.

But gradually the numbers whittled themselves down to a steady group of about six, and it was a delightful group to work with.

There were two retired ladies in their sixties, one a former teacher, the other a chemist. The teacher had a pen-friend in the States and a daughter who lived in England, so her basic English was good. The chemist loved to travel, especially to the far East, where often English was the easiest common language. Her vocabulary and grammar were good, her accent needed a little work.

There was a woman in her forties, who had learned English to degree level and wasn't bad, though not as good as she thought she was. She couldn't resist giving everyone the benefit of her opinion. If one of the others asked me a question, she would often chip in with her answer first, invariably wrong, and it took a lot of tact on my part to correct her diplomatically.

Then there was an army officer, in his fifties, who needed to improve his English to a level where he could interact with other NATO troops – OTAN, in French, which always made me think of a character or a place from a Tolkien story. He was a delightful pupil, very keen and eager to learn, with a great sense of humour, who brought a lot to our little group.

He told us he'd been going to a language school in Clermont and paying more than eighty euros a session, spending almost eighty percent of the time being lectured in French about English grammar. He was delighted that Rule No. 1 of my little group was 'No French Spoken Here'.

I was very strict with the English only rule, as it's the only way to learn a language. I started a swear box – anyone heard speaking French had to put a few coppers in a little box. And I was sneaky, too. If I heard my pupils coming up the garden steps speaking French, I would rush out rattling the little box.

In principle, I made no charge for the group. I wanted to give something back to the country which had so far welcomed us with open arms. And I really wanted to do something to redress the bad reputation of so many Brit ex-pats for taking without giving. I left it entirely open to my pupils if they wanted to give me a little something in exchange. I said I was perfectly happy to have cake, chocolates, anything they wanted to barter. I also left out a little dish so they could, if they wished, leave a small cash donation, which most of them usually did. It helped cover the cost of the paper and computer ink for the print-outs I created every week for the current lesson.

For a time we had a very nice older teenage girl who needed to improve her English to become a flight attendant. But she moved house, and her place was taken by two teenage girls, sisters, one nearly seventeen when she started with us, one nearly fifteen.

It was absolutely wonderful to have such a mixed group, and the girls said they were surprised and delighted to feel they were being treated as equals. We discussed the differences in French and British culture, covering a wide range of subjects, and I always asked the girls for their input, so we had a different perspective.

We played lateral thinking games, the sort where you're given a set of facts and by asking closed questions to which the only answers are yes or no, you arrive at a logical conclusion. You know the sort of thing: there's a dead body, two pieces of wood and some sawdust. You have to establish why, not how, the body died. If you don't know that one, you'll now be wracking your brains for the solution – sorry!

The activity I enjoyed the most was our weekly Show and Tell. I got the idea from the Peanuts cartoons, it being more of an American activity than a typically English one, but it was a great way to get my pupils talking.

Each week they would be asked to bring an object of their own choosing and tell us all about it and what it meant to them. We had some really original and interesting talks. Our army officer came resplendent in full mess kit with kilt, since his regiment had Irish connections.

The older teenager brought her flute and played for us, the younger brought her accordion and played that. But the most entertaining and original of all came from our former teacher.

She arrived with a small cardboard box with a wide slit in the top, the sort used to dispense paper handkerchiefs. It was beautifully decorated in green shamrocks and over the top of the slit was a piece of fine green chiffon. When we peeped inside, we found small bright centime coins, a tiny little stool and a miniature silver bucket, all in dolls' house scale. None of us could guess what it was.

It was, she told us, a leprechaun trap. She was fascinated by Celtic folklore and had read of such things. Leprechauns, she told us, were attracted by shiny coins, hence the centimes, and by ale, represented by the little bucket. The leprechauns would come along, drawn by the coins and the beer, stand on the chiffon, then fall through the slit as it gave way. Finding themselves trapped, they would sit on the stool and drink the beer, being unable to escape. They could then be held prisoner and made to disclose the legendary crock of gold at the end of the rainbow, which all leprechauns are said to know about. What a delightful story!

At this time, I had decided to study for a TEFL qualification, Teaching English as a Foreign Language, so I would have another skill to fall back on, should I ever need it. I was doing a distance learning course and had to submit papers for marking, on various subjects set by the tutors.

I was not, it has to be said, very impressed with the course overall. I have always firmly believed, when learning a new language, it is best to learn from someone who speaks it correctly themselves, without too much slang or poor grammar – though not necessarily French from a *parisienne!* Once you have a good basic grasp, you can easily slip into whatever regional accent you want to suit where you live, so you can order *paing* instead of *pain* (bread) if you live in the south of France, for example.

When I lived in Wales and was learning Welsh, I chose a local vicar as my teacher, knowing his Welsh was likely to be correct. I'm not the only one who makes mistakes with language – the vicar lived in the small village of Llanfihangel-ar-ardd, which a Londoner, new to the area, once pronounced as Laughing Angels in Art.

So I was fairly horrified when one of the training videos which accompanied the course told us we should teach English colloquially and with whatever accent we had. The TEFL teacher featured on the video had his pupils reciting in unison 'he use'ter live in a cassstle' which made me cringe, having never knowingly said 'use-ter' in my life. Those of you who have read *Sell the Pig* will know I am an unashamed snob.

The paper I was currently writing for my TEFL qualification involved describing a game which would be suitable for English learners, and since Show and Tell worked so well for mine, I decided to use it as an example and cite the lovely leprechaun trap.

Those courses are geared largely for students off on a gap year wanting to teach English to earn money to fund their back-packing. I'm not sure who the tutors are who mark the papers, but they probably aren't used to a grumpy old wordsmith submitting a paper and taking issue with their comments on it.

The paper called for a game, so I cited our Show and Tell. The tutor wrote that whilst it was no doubt an amusing activity, they weren't sure if it was an actual game.

Harrumph!

I think I was probably born clutching a copy of The Oxford Dictionary of English. It has certainly hardly left my hand since.

I emailed them back with Oxford's definition of game: 'an activity that one engages in for amusement' and suggested, as politely as I could, that if they were going to make comments on use of English, they should at least familiarise themselves with Oxford before making fatuous remarks. I know – I'm the pupil from hell!

My contact with my English pupils was to be the start of a long friendship with many of them. Our army officer moved on – a two-year tour in Afghanistan – but before he left, he called on me and showered me with gifts as he was thrilled with the progress he had made - he had passed the necessary English exams with ease. His gifts were so generous and thoughtful and showed how much he had listened and taken in about me. They included little pastries from Luxembourg and a *stöllen*, the traditional German Christmas treat, as a reminder of my four years in Germany.

The contact with French friends helped me a lot with my grasp of the language. I still, of course, made errors. Discussing the improvement in Mother's appetite with the carers, I enthusiastically told them she was eating like a bone these days. Except, of course, I meant eating like a bear, muddling up *os* and *ours*.

But then such mistakes are not limited to dealing in foreign languages. I know of people getting just as caught out by unfamiliar regional accents in the British Isles.

A friend of mine, relatively well spoken, in a southern English sort of way, found himself in the Midlands and, having a headache, he trotted off to the nearest Boots the chemist and asked for some aspirin.

"Ferinadol?" the young lady behind the counter asked him.

Being unfamiliar with the brand name he said: "No, just ordinary aspirin will be fine."

"Yes," said the assistant patiently, "but is it fer an adul' or fer a child?"

Chapter Ten
How Green Was My Tuk-Tuk

My brother has always been very into the notion of being green. It's ironic, since in many ways he is one of the most extravagant and wasteful people I know. But the intentions are there, and he's always embracing new greener technology and investigating things like domestic solar power and wind power.

He decided he simply had to have an electric car. So he bought one, sight unseen, on eBay. Like you do. He also bought it without really thinking through, not just the practicalities of owning and running one in the middle of nowhere, but also the logistics of going and collecting it from Bordeaux, some four hundred kilometres away.

He first favoured going down in the removals lorry he had bought to transport our furniture out to France, and winching it up the ramp somehow, until I pointed out the two obvious flaws in that plan.

Firstly, it was a drop-tail lorry, so even once winched up the ramp, the electric car would require some sort of hydraulic lift to get it up the drop from the ramp to the inner floor.

Secondly, my brother told me the electric car, a Renault Clio, was very heavy as, despite having no engine, just an electric motor, the battery which powered it was very heavy indeed. This meant a lot of weight would be concentrated over a very small area over the back wheels, whereas a furniture van, with its plywood floor, was designed to have its load fairly spread about. So there was a little uncertainty in my mind over whether the floor would bear the weight.

The autonomy of the vehicle was no more than eighty kilometres on a maximum charge. They were designed for in-town driving rather than long haul, so driving it back was out of the question; it would have taken a week with stops to recharge the battery en route.

I pointed out that the Dingley, the Hymer motorhome, was quite a hefty beast, well up to towing and fitted with a tow hitch. I suggested my brother hire a small trailer, the sort designed to transport ride-on mowers and the like, and go and collect it with that. I pointed out that there was a hire depot in the nearby town of Riom which seemed to hire most things, so I proposed contacting them and booking a trailer for the trip.

My brother decided he didn't feel quite confident enough to do the whole adventure himself, so once again we called on the driving skills of our friend Young Bobby, who agreed to come over with my brother and do the Bordeaux trip to collect the car.

Organisation has never been one of my brother's strong points and this was turning into another exercise of fox, chicken, corn, river. For those who don't know it and haven't read *Sell the Pig*, that's the brain exercise where you have to find a way to transport a fox, a chicken and some corn across a river in a boat which only holds two of them at a time, without ever leaving the fox alone with the chicken, or the chicken alone with the corn.

For reasons of his own, my brother never got round to ordering a trailer locally, and had instead hired one down in Bordeaux, so his and YB's itinerary was going to look like this:

Thursday: drive over from Wales to the Pink House
Friday: drive down to Bordeaux to collect a trailer, load the car, and have a rest
Saturday: drive back from Bordeaux with car, then return to Bordeaux
Sunday: drive back from Bordeaux having dropped off the trailer.

The little car duly arrived. I'm not quite sure what I expected, but the first thing that surprised me was that it was about ten or twelve years old – I hadn't realised electric cars had been around for as long as that.

It was a little white car and looked like any other older Clio on the road except it was almost totally silent when running, just a very faint hum like a quiet washing machine on the spin cycle. It didn't go very fast, but it was very cheap to run, just plug it into the mains circuit whenever the battery needed a top up.

I took it for a little spin about to get the feel of it, since I was to be allowed to play with it to take Mother out on green trips, thus saving me money on diesel. It was an automatic, so very easy to drive, and I quickly nick-named it the tuk-tuk.

Poor YB had done all the driving on their to-ing and fro-ing so was in need of a well-earned break, so I took him away with me on my R&R. I'd discovered a campsite which I quite liked, despite its seemingly urban situation.

It was in the very pukka spa town of Royat, on the outskirts of Clermont-Ferrand, and was in a much higher price range than my usual choice of site, but it did have a nice swimming pool and it was well laid out. The pitches were tucked away in wooded areas, well separated from one another, so it had a pleasantly rural feel.

Sadly, because of the arthritis affecting my thumbs, I'd had to give up using my nice trailer tent. It had extending poles with a little stud that popped out to keep them extended. To take it down involved having to press the spring-loaded studs in with your thumbs, and there was quite a bit of resistance. I simply could not do that on some days and since I favoured campsites with very few people about, and it was utterly impossible to drive the trailer without first folding the tent away, I'd had to stop using it when by myself.

Instead, I'd discovered a wonderful new modern invention, the two-second pop-up tent. What a brilliant idea! You literally just unzipped the bag, undid the retaining strap and pop! You had a fully functioning and very good tent in the promised two seconds. I was thrilled skinny with my purchase, and the first time I tried it out was at the Royat site.

I had a moment's sadness, thinking how much Meic would have loved to see the tent pop up. As I put my camping chair outside it and settled down with a cup of tea, a little owl flew past. It's a type of owl, *Athene noctua*, not just an owl of small stature. They are quite often seen in daylight, and this made a very low, very slow pass quite close to my new tent, for all the world as if it was most impressed with what it was looking at.

So I took YB to Royat and let him play with my pop-up tent whilst I used my trusty old Eurohike. I'm not much of a swimmer by nature, having only learned comparatively late on in life, but as the cost of the site was so much higher than my usual budget, I was determined to have a splash about in the pool. Probably sensibly, since it was not all that warm, YB preferred to sit on the terrace, drink lager and watch.

After that YB drove my brother back to Wales and I planned a first little outing for me and Mother in the tuk-tuk, as we were invited to a wedding in a few weeks time and I thought it would make a better form of transport than my scruffy old van.

The wedding in question was that of our favourite carer, Lili. She was marrying her long-term partner with whom she had lived for some time, having built a house together and had a son with him. As she said, she liked to do things the opposite way round to most people.

Mother and I would only be going to see Lili leave the church, as I thought any more would be a bit tiring and confusing for Mother. But we were thrilled to be asked to be there, and I bundled Mother into the tuk-tuk the day before and took her for a nice hairdo. I spent some time with her sorting out what she was going to wear for the occasion and collecting petals from the roses in the garden that we could throw at Lili when she emerged from the church.

France is a secular country, contrary to what many people believe, with an absence of religious involvement in government affairs and vice versa. So only civil weddings are officially recognised, and these take place in the *mairie*, the town hall, performed by the mayor or another civil servant. Some couples chose to have a church ceremony as well, as Lili did.

It was a beautiful sunny day, just perfect for a wedding. Lili emerged from the church looking radiant. She had lost her mother when she was only a teenager, but all the rest of her family and friends were there, so it was particularly touching that she hurried across to see her *mamie anglaise*, greeting her with a big hug and kisses, and posing for lots of photos with her.

Mother was thrilled. Lili was one of the few new people in her life she always recognised and there was a real close bond between the two of them, just like blood-related grandmother and grand-daughter.

Lili's forthcoming honeymoon to Portugal was one of the reasons I was still dogless – I had agreed to look after her little *toutou* whilst she went away, as there was no-one else who could do it. So I'd decided to leave replacing Meic until after that, and after my summer round of visitors.

I'd discovered the French word *toutou*, or doggy, the first time Meic and I had stayed in an hotel together. On one R&R day, it was absolutely siling down, as they say oop north, (translation note for southerners: raining very heavily!) with no signs of stopping, and even I didn't fancy a night in a tent. So I decided to treat us to a night in an hotel, and chose the fairly inexpensive but very clean and friendly one at Issoire where my brother and I had stayed on our second house-hunting trip to the Auvergne, the one on which we had found and chosen the Pink House.

Most hotels, and most campsites in the region, accepted dogs with no problem. I had only found one campsite in the whole *Puy de Dôme département* which did not. But just in case, I left Meic in the van while I went in to reception and asked if they had a room available for me and my dog.

The very charming but rather camp young man on the desk said: "A room for you and your *toutou?* But of course, *madame*."

I had to sneakily check my pocket dictionary to see if *toutou* was an acceptable word. But I increasingly heard it used so started to adopt it myself. Many French are just as soft and soppy about their pets as are some English. I'd already started phoning the vet to book appointments for my *toutou*, or my *minette*, my doggy or my pussy cat.

There was something of a fashion, especially in that area, to have pseudo-English names for shops and businesses. So, for example, a dog beauty parlour I'd seen was called Toutou Much. A lot of English words were creeping into the French language, not all of them correctly used.

At the hairdresser, I'd booked Mother in for *un brushing*, which is actually a cut and blow-dry. I could imagine that if one asked for a *brushing* in a UK hairdresser, one might be told quite firmly to go and brush one's own hair.

Not long after Meic died, Jill came out for her annual visit. We were planning to go away for the week and as she never minded much where we went, as long as it was quiet and peaceful, I asked her if she'd be happy if we went to the same campsite in the Massif du Sancy where Meic spent his last night.

I'd already been back once. It helped me to come to terms with the loss I was still feeling to be somewhere we had had fun together, before the end. Whilst there, I'd had the most bizarre experience, for which I have no logical explanation – you must draw your own conclusions.

I was walking in the hills where Meic and I had walked many times together, with him always trotting along beside my left leg. It was a beautiful sunny day and I was strolling along enjoying the warmth and the smells of the many wild flowers.

Then I noticed that as I walked, there was a distinct shadow, moving along beside my left leg. A trick of the light? Possibly. Yet I was not casting any shadow, and the sun was not in the right place to account for it. It gave me the most incredibly warm feeling, though the phenomenon, whatever it was, sadly never repeated itself.

Despite some fairly dire weather, Jill and I had a brilliant time, as ever. I still had the trailer tent, even though I could no longer use it by myself, so with Jill's strong thumbs to help dismantle it, we took that, with the intention that Jill could have the bedroom and I would sleep in the awning. As it turned out, it rained so hard and so persistently that there was a small stream perpetually running through the awning so I had to sleep in the back of the van.

On one particularly wet day, deciding we couldn't be any wetter if we tried, we went into the smart spa town of La Bourboule, a great favourite holiday destination with the French, and spent some time relaxing in a warm jacuzzi and occasionally doing a couple of languid lengths of a small swimming pool.

Driving back from the town to our campsite, we spotted a hairdresser with one of those pseudo-English names. 'Fanny Feeling'. I assure you, it really was called that, it's not a typo. We started laughing so uncontrollably, especially at the thought of what that could conjure up as an entry in someone's diary, that I very nearly crashed the van.

Apart from dog-sitting Lili's *toutou*, I had decided to stay dogless for a while because I was to have another visit from my old school friend Meg and I didn't think it fair to inflict a new dog on her when we went off camping, in case it was one with problems which needed to be sorted out.

Meg was recently divorced from her husband of more than thirty years and with a new partner. The partner, and his son, were driving down, dropping her off at the Pink House and going off by themselves to do a mountaineering holiday. Meg would stay a few days then I'd take her to the station and put her on a train to go and visit a friend in another part of France.

Having the tuk-tuk meant I could take her and Mother both out on little trips together, which I had been unable to do the previous year with only the single passenger-seated van.

I'd gone out with Meg's brother Cedric, always known as Cedge, for about sixth months when we were both in sixth form and had remained in erratic contact with him. He now lived in Australia but was visiting Europe and managed to arrange a flying visit to the Pink House at the same time, as he had not yet met Meg's new man.

Meg and I were going to go camping for my R&R and had planned to walk up the Puy de Dôme volcano. Lili's little *toutou* was a wee Yorkshire, not much used to long walks, so he was to be left behind under the eye of the carers who would be looking after Mother.

Obviously with Lili away on her honeymoon, she wouldn't be in charge of Mother, but the team in place was largely a good one, although as always, there were one or two who were not as good as the others. There was the rather loopy Lucy who could not grasp at all Mother's lack of memory and kept asking her questions based on things she'd told her days before. And who one morning decided to get the atlas out and start giving Mother a lesson on French geography instead of putting her on the commode as she was supposed to.

Meg and I had a great time. We took the longer, more leisurely route to climb the Puy, rather than the direct but punishingly steep mule track which is much shorter. The summit, as always, was very busy with tourists, being one of France's most visited attractions.

After our little break, we took advantage of the tuk-tuk to take Mother out on a few little trips so she could show Meg 'Billinge Lump'. And after Meg left, I used it quite a bit to take Mother out and about to do all sorts of necessary trips, like taking her to the doctor or *pharmacie*, and, very importantly, taking her for a new hearing aid.

My old van was right-hand drive, so Mother, in the passenger seat, got very anxious, seemingly always being in the path of oncoming traffic. The tuk-tuk was left-hand drive, which put her at the side of the road and made it much more pleasant for her. The concept of using the clean, green energy appealed to me very much, so we happily trundled about in it when we could.

The only time I could do any shopping was if I took Mother with me, which I tried to do whenever I could, or, if I didn't feel up to manhandling her on a particular day, I would whiz down to our local town, about three miles away, whilst the morning carer was attending to Mother.

It was cutting it very fine, as there was only just enough time to get there, shop and get back again. If it involved a trip to the *pharmacie* as well, I was always on pins as they were so nice in there and always took time to talk to everyone, that it was never a flying visit.

I'd noticed early on that there were almost never queues of people in the medical centre waiting room to see the doctor. But pharmacists here have such an important role and carry it out so well they are usually the preferred first port of call for illness, which takes a huge burden off the doctors.

One morning I was on a whiz to collect a prescription – well, strictly speaking, it wasn't possible to whiz in the tuk-tuk, more of a sedate glide – and as I was going down the hill towards town, the motor suddenly just cut out. Nothing. Zippo. Zilch. No familiar washing machine hum.

And I was struck with the major flaw in this wonderful plan of being greener. In the event of a breakdown, there was absolutely no way of getting the tuk-tuk going again as I could with my van, which had become an increasingly dodgy starter. With the van, I could simply roll it a bit and bump start it. Or use the very good portable jump-start kit I'd invested in.

But the tuk-tuk wouldn't bump start. It had no engine to prod back into life and no conventional battery to connect jump leads to. Once it stopped, that was it. And I highly doubted if our little local garage, good though they were, would have the first clue of how to get an electric tuk-tuk going again.

Ever the optimist, I turned the key once more and was immediately rewarded by the familiar purring hum; I put it in drive and we went on our way. Phew! I was hoping it was just a loose connection somewhere that had wiggled about a bit going over a bump.

I mentioned the problem to my brother, of course, but he, like me, assumed and hoped it was just a passing glitch, and for quite some time afterwards, the tuk-tuk continued to purr and glide obediently, so I could take Mother on lots of little outings.

A big part of rural French life is the *vide grenier* season. A *vide grenier* is like an attic sale, or a car boot sale, though often without the cars where space was limited. Most of the small towns round about have at least one a year and the season goes from about Easter to the end of summer, depending on the weather.

Some are huge affairs, with refreshments and even a funfair. Some are modest, with maybe half a dozen tables.

The quality of what's on offer also varies enormously, from really good stuff at bargain prices to absolute tat at ridiculously inflated prices which no-one pays. The best traders are those who go with the sensible idea that they are there to *débarrasser*, to clear out, and pitch their prices accordingly. They are the ones who finish the day with largely empty tables and full purses.

When Mother lived in Cheshire, she and her best friend Ruby were the demon queens of the jumble sales. It was like a military operation. As soon as the local weekly paper came out, Mother would go through the adverts, red pen in hand, and mark all the jumble sales within their range. Then with her A-Z of the area, she would find the exact locations and draw up a list of possibles.

Ruby was the driver, so she had the final say on which ones they went to. She was also not a morning person, so they had to be afternoons for her. If Mother fancied any of the morning ones, she would go along herself on the bus, if feasible.

Whenever I went to stay with Mother, I would do the driving and take them both to as many as we could manage. I think our record was six in one day.

My brother would also happily chauffeur them to the jumblies when he was visiting. And as his eclectic and eccentric collection of vehicles included a vintage Rolls Royce Silver Shadow, in British racing green, that was his preferred method of transporting them.

Jumble sales, for those who have never been, are hugely popular in many areas and it's not at all unusual to find queues of people halfway down the road waiting to get in to the good ones. And Cheshire, being one of the richest counties in England, has some wonderful ones.

It always created quite a stir when my brother's Rolls glided up outside the venue, he stepped out, wearing the chauffeur's cap he favoured when playing the part, and opened the back doors to let the two elderly ladies descend, clutching their supply of bin bags and all ready to rummage.

Central France generally having a better climate than most parts of the UK, the *vide greniers* are almost always outside, with tables lining the street. They usually begin early morning, around seven o'clock, and go on till six or seven in the evening. So there is no need to queue, one just turns up and starts to go round the stalls.

One of the great mysteries to me about rural French living has always been: do the French have different bladders to the English? The lack of public conveniences in many of these small towns has always made me wonder how the average French person manages. Often even a medium sized supermarket will have no loos for the use of its customers. So the only choice is to go into a café, where one usually feels obliged to buy a drink, which makes it an expensive way to spend a penny.

Sometimes there are Portaloos available at the *vide greniers*, and one or two of the towns and visitor attractions in the region are now installing composting toilets, perfect for year-round use as they require no water connection, so nothing to freeze up in the often very cold winters of parts of the Massif Central.

It wasn't a problem with Mother. She had long since lost bladder control so always wore what the carers called *"pool-oops"*, pull-up training type pants which dealt effectively and discreetly with any little accidents. I was sometimes tempted to try them myself when going to somewhere with a distinct lack of a loo.

Mother loved the *vide greniers*. She still had a brilliant eye for a quality bargain, but also had an almost child-like fascination for cuddly toys. I'd heard of homes for the elderly in the UK which refused to allow residents' families to bring in toys, saying it was demeaning for the elderly residents.

What a load of rubbish! Mother always snuggled down for the night with Baby, her almost life-size toy collie, which looked so like Meic it used to make the carers jump when they saw it on the bed, her little teddy in a pretty pink dressing gown, and washed out old Blue Ted, a favourite from childhood days of my brother and me.

One day at a *vide grenier* she spotted a toy which looked for all the world like a small German shepherd puppy, and she wanted it. As is traditional at such events, I haggled vigorously over the price and secured it for all of fifty centimes. Mother was in her wheelchair, of course, so I pushed her around with the toy, which she named Tinker, on her knee, and several people stopped to look at the 'puppy'.

We always arrived home from the *vide grenier* with bag-loads of new treasures to unpack, sort and put in the washing machine. The tuk-tuk continued behaving beautifully for a while, ferrying us to and fro on these little weekly trips we both enjoyed so much,

Unfortunately the tuk-tuk's exemplary conduct didn't last indefinitely and the sudden cut-outs became much more common, to the extent that I didn't feel confident to drive it, certainly not when taking Mother out, and had to go back to using my polluting but more trusty old van.

My brother continued to use the tuk-tuk to run around in but then he started having the same problems with it so decided to get it seen to. I think I would have been inclined to check out the repair situation before embarking on buying a still unusual vehicle, as he then found out that the nearest place to get it repaired was in Clermont-Ferrand, which was about at the limit of its autonomy, when it was being unreliable. That meant it always had to go in for at least twenty-four hours so it could be recharged again overnight.

It was in and out of the garage seemingly endlessly, trying to fix an intermittent problem, always the most difficult to diagnose and repair. And because my brother was still dividing his time between the Pink House and his place in Wales, it fell to me to have to keep phoning the garage and haranguing them for their lack of progress.

Although my French was improving all the time, learning mechanical terminology was challenging, especially as I didn't know the words for the parts of an electric car in English, never mind French. But I managed to understand that some major part needed re-grinding or re-boring and that there was only one place in the whole of France which could do it. The offending part had gone away to them for attention but it could be months and months before it was fixed and returned.

So the tuk-tuk was to spend more of its time off the road than on - the little white Clio was proving to be a bit of a white elephant in disguise.

Chapter Eleven
A Four-Legged Friend

When pupils at my junior school were discussing their future careers – gender stereotypical nursing for the girls, engineering for the boys – I only ever wanted to be a cowboy. Never a cowgirl, just a cowboy.

My earliest records were not pop groups or the boy bands of the day but singing cowboys Roy Rogers and Gene Autry. And my favourite track of all time was 'A Four-legged Friend.'

'He's honest and faithful right up to the end, that wonderful one-two-three-four-legged friend,' ran the lyrics, and that was so true of my old friend Meic.

After nearly eight months without him or any other dog in my life, I still missed him more than I would have thought possible.

Not all of my friends truly understood the yawning void in my life. Penny accused me of 'wallowing'. I was trying not to, but I was hurting, deeply. And my health was being affected. My weight was up and down like a yo-yo, totally uncharacteristic for me.

I tried to keep up my tradition of evening walks while the carers were with mother, but without a dog by my side, I struggled to find the motivation. And similarly on my R&R days, although Meic couldn't walk all that far, we did at least between us go for plenty of gentle strolls. Without a dog, I was spending too much time sitting in the sun with my nose in a book.

It was time to do something about it.

I decided I wanted to adopt an unwanted dog rather than get a pedigree. I'd done it once before with little Mady, a collie cross, and she had been one of the best and easiest dogs I'd ever owned.

In my mind's eye, I saw myself walking the hills I loved with a calm, obedient, young female non-collie breed in glorious golden colours. I decided that after four collies and a collie cross, it was time for something completely different.

France has humane societies, just like the UK, and I knew there was a large SPA, *Société Protectrice des Animaux*, refuge not far from the Pink House. I started keeping an eye on their website to see if there was anything that seemed suitable.

It was the same depressing tale of animal woe as in many refuges in Britain, far too many animals, crammed into pens, far too few people coming forward to adopt them. An awful lot of the dogs there were hunting dogs which had strayed during the hunt, were not identified with chip, tattoo or collar and no-one came forward to claim them. Some had been in the kennels for literally years.

I didn't see anything that really took my eye. There were some border collies, a hugely popular breed in France, but I really wanted something a bit different.

Hippy Chick was a dog lover. She had an ancient English setter, was getting herself a young Great Dane and had just adopted a little collie cross, a real bundle of mischief, from the SPA for her son. She told me she knew the people at the refuge so would be happy to go along with me to see if we could find something suitable.

Our visit was the day after their *portes ouvertes* (open doors) weekend, which I thought meant that the best and easiest of the dogs would have been snapped up and what was left and not reserved was likely to be the older, the uglier, and the dogs with behavioural issues. But I was getting desperate for a dog, so off we went.

The noise level was truly deafening. There were dogs packed two and three to a run and it seemed that every one of the hundred or so in there was barking and yelping at the top of its voice as we walked up and down the row of cages.

We were looking at the big and medium sized dogs as I didn't think I was yet ready to have a toy or a lapdog. There was nothing remotely like what I was looking for.

There was one border collie, a very black dog, none of the common white face markings of the breed, but with smart white stockings to its front legs. It was a male, sharing a pen with a small indeterminate breed and seemingly afraid of it. As we passed, the collie was barking frenziedly and showing lots of teeth, so we carried on walking.

The only thing that remotely fitted any of the criteria I had gone with was a young black Labrador cross female, just about a year old, but who had had no training of any description. Although friendly, she looked as mad as a box of frogs, possibly not the ideal choice to share a house with a frail old lady of ninety.

We went in search of the lady in charge, the one Hippy Chick knew, to ask if there were any other dogs secreted about the premises anywhere, or if she could suggest something which might fit my criteria: female, not more than a year old, golden or sandy coloured and not a border collie.

Mrs Dog Assigner asked if I would consider a border collie, if it was the right dog. I explained that I had already owned four and had recently lost one to whom I was incredibly attached and wasn't sure if the time was right to get another.

She said they did have a collie in, a male, only two years old, but he was having a dreadful time in kennels, not coping at all well, and desperately needed to be out of there, if they could find someone with collie experience to give him a good home.

She told us he'd had a very good home, been extremely well looked after, and then whoops, the couple who owned him were suddenly having a baby – where did that come from? - and could no longer cope with the dog. So they did the very worst thing it's possible to do to an intelligent and sensitive dog like a collie – they drove him to the refuge and signed him over to them.

The dog had been absolutely devastated at the betrayal and was not doing well in the refuge. She asked if I would at least take a look at him. Inevitably, she led us to the kennel with the barking, snarling black dog.

His name, the card on the gate told us, was Quartz, but in French it's pronounced in a rather harsh way, more like Kwatss, so that it sounded like a Klingon swear word. And he looked about as angry as a Klingon who'd just been taken prisoner aboard the Star Ship Enterprise.

The lady assured us that, once outside the pen which he hated, he was a different dog entirely, very nicely behaved and friendly, and suggested Hippy Chick and I took him and his kennel companion out for a little walk around to see what I thought.

Indeed, as soon as leads were found and we got the two dogs out of their cage and outside the refuge for a walk along the track, Quartz truly was a different dog. He play-bowed to my feet, his tail wagging, his face mischievous, those brown eyes looking up at me in that: 'Are you going to be my new *maitresse?*' way.

Oh dear. I was hooked. How could I put a dog like that back into the pen which was obviously slowing frying his brains?

I'd gone with the specific agenda of finding a one-year-old bitch with a golden coat, of any breeding other than collie. So how did I find myself driving away with a two-year-old black and white male border collie in the back of my van?

Adopting from the SPA is an expensive business. The cost to adopt a dog like Quartz was two hundred and forty euros, but that did include microchipping, vaccination and neutering. Although in his case, he was already chipped and fully vaccinated, but not castrated.

And as it turned out, he was a cryptorchid, one testicle had not descended into the scrotum, so a simple, straight-forward castration was not possible, it would need abdominal surgery. That was essential, as the condition carries a greatly increased risk of testicular cancer. Of course, the SPA would only pay the normal cost of basic castration, I would have to pay the difference.

There was no home visit or inspection, they simply did not have the resources to carry them out, but they asked detailed questions and were happy to take Happy Chick's word for it that I would provide a suitable home.

The next step was to take Quartz back to the Pink House on a week's trial, to see if we would suit one another.

He jumped happily into Meic's travel cage in the back of the van and was beautifully behaved on the journey, no barking or dashing about as some collies do when travelling. He seemed to sense that this was a test which he needed to pass.

I wasn't staying out for the night on this R&R, I'd already decided it was not a good idea with a brand new dog in tow, inflicting my eccentric camping lifestyle on it without knowing anything about it. So we were going back to the Pink House but I would be off duty and would sleep up in the top flat, leaving the duty carer to see to Mother.

Hippy Chick's brother now often did the night shift on my nights off. I personally thought him a bit of a twit, because the first time he did a night, he totally failed to check that the baby alarm was plugged in, so had no way of hearing if Mother needed attention or not.

Hippy Chick had assured us that the carers in my absence, especially the night shift, were all very experienced, so I rather assumed that meant qualified in some way. It certainly sounded as if her brother had some qualifications as when I arrived back, he was talking to Lili about the requirements to pass the next level of exam up to go from *aide à domicile* (home help) to *aide soignante* (care assistant).

I did think it strange that someone supposedly experienced could manage to go the whole night without realising the baby alarm wasn't on. Little old ladies, even when passing a peaceful night, are very seldom silent, and Mother's snoring usually resonated around the house, even without the aid of the baby alarm. But I was prepared to let it go the once, having been assured it was a one-off.

I took Quartz into the sitting room, where Lili was handing over to Hippy Chick's brother, and he quietly and politely introduced himself to them with none of the aggressive barking I had seen at the refuge. It was looking good.

We spent an uneventful week. Quartz was on his best behaviour and didn't put a paw wrong. He pulled a bit on the lead but not drastically, he knew the command to sit and stay and showed an aptitude for learning and a willingness to please. His coat was magnificent, full and shiny and beautifully groomed. He had clearly been extremely well looked after, which must have made his abandonment even harder for him to come to terms with. There was absolutely no question of me taking him back to the refuge where he had been so desperately unhappy.

I decided to change his name, although some people consider it unlucky. He didn't seem to respond particularly to Quartz, and anyway it was such a harsh word it sounded as if I was telling him off. I can never resist a play on words, so I decided to call him Ci, which is the Welsh word for dog, and is pronounced 'key', so sounds exactly like the French word *qui*, who.

This was going to lead to some amusing exchanges:

"Comment s'appelle votre chien?" (What is your dog called?)

"Ci", sounding like *"Qui?"* (who?)

"Votre chien," (your dog)

"Ci," and so on. A bit like the old Abbot and Costello sketch, 'Who's on first base'.

The first R&R Ci and I spent together was another hotel trip. He must have thought he'd landed well and truly on his paws. It was just that I'd done a bit of copy editing work as a freebie for an old friend but she had insisted on paying me and had sent me all the leftover euros in her purse at the end of a European trip, so I'd decided to treat myself.

Hippy Chick had been telling me about the town of Saint Nectaire in the Massif du Sancy, and how in its glory days in the sixties it had been a mecca for rich Russians wanting to take the waters and the mountain air. Apparently it had now fallen from favour as the financial crisis started to bite far and wide, so was more like a ghost town, with lots of empty property, some of which had been for sale for years, decades, probably. It sounded intriguing.

With my spending money in my pocket, I decided to reward myself with a night in its main hotel, taking Ci with me, of course. I also wanted to check out the area as YB was coming back shortly for a visit and bringing with him my old and dear friend Alex, and I wanted to take them somewhere nice on my R&R days.

Ci was quite a nervous little dog, and he was quite small for a collie, especially compared to Meic who had been a big, solid dog. It was clear he was not used to the sort of mad adventures I favoured, so his new life was going to be a bit of a learning curve. And it began with taking the lift up to our room in the hotel.

The strange sensation of the lift floor swaying and moving under his paws was bad enough. But the disembodied male voice telling him the floor numbers was nearly too much for him.

I was really looking forward to luxuriating in a bath in my hotel room, since I only ever took showers at the Pink House. Water is metered in France, so for economy I didn't use the bath, especially as it was a big one and took a lot to fill.

The hotel advertised a swimming pool and a sauna, and my room was supposed to have a bath. The pool, when I went to investigate, was a tiny one, and as there was a family with lots of noisy kids already using it, I did nothing more than dip myself in it after sitting in the sauna.

My bath was tiny. I'm not tall, only five feet four, and it was too short for me. Worse, it was the last week in October, at an altitude of two and a half thousand feet and the bathroom heater was not working.

I trotted down to the reception desk to report it, and a young man came back up with me to see if he could fix it.

Ci was not at all keen on allowing a strange man into the room. He had already decided that his new mission in life was to defend me, to the death if necessary. Luckily, I had invested in a Dog Bag, a sort of portable pop-up tent for dogs, in which he could be zipped and confined, after a fashion. Outdoors, it could be pegged down like a proper tent and held in place, but inside a bedroom, it was tending to move about a bit as he lunged and barked ferociously, making the young man very nervous.

The man discovered he could not fix the wall heater – the pull chord seemed to have come adrift and was not switching on the heat. So he instead produced a fan heater for me.

As I lay, or rather, squatted, in my short bath, I wondered yet again about the difference in French and English attitudes to Health and Safety, as I sat with an electric fan heater plugged into an open socket in a bathroom, balanced perilously close to my bath.

If Ci thought all our R&Rs were going to be spent in an hotel, he was in for a rude awakening. The next week on my day off, I took him wild camping in the back of the van. Most of the campsites in the area closed for business from September to Easter, at the earliest, and many of them were only open for the high season. So because I liked to go away every week for a little break, I often found myself sleeping in the van in some strange and remote places.

That week we went to a nearby reservoir and parked up at the side of a track leading down to it. The police were always very vigilant in such areas, making sure no-one was fishing where they did not have permission to, and that no-one was hunting where they shouldn't, either.

I didn't try to hide the van away in a corner when I slept in it, as I thought that looked furtive and suspicious. I just parked up in the quietest, most level spot I could find that didn't appear to be on private property. I still hadn't quite mastered the art of telling what was public or private, so I tended to go on the theory that if it was not specifically labelled as *propriété privée*, I was probably safe enough parking there, and certainly nobody ever disturbed or challenged me on my little nocturnal adventures.

On this particular morning, after Ci and I had enjoyed a good and undisturbed sleep in the cosy back of the van, I'd put him out in the Dog Bag, roughly pegged out by just a couple of corners, to have his breakfast, whilst I was in the back of the van having a bit of a wash and changing into clean undies.

I heard a car coming down the track just as I was half into clean knickers. Ci immediately launched into a furious barking frenzy, clearly threatening to rip limb from limb anyone who dared to approach his *maitresse*, especially when she was in a state of undress.

Peering out from under the curtain covering the back window, whilst still trying to wriggle into my kecks, I saw with a sinking heart, a *gendarmerie* vehicle coming down the track towards us. At the same time I saw Ci, still inside his Dog Bag, start determinedly trying to race towards the approaching car like some sort of giant hamster in a sturdy nylon wheel.

Mentally trying to calculate which of my possible crimes carried the stiffest penalty– illegal camping, being the owner of a dangerous dog clearly out of control, or indecent exposure in front of *gendarmes* – I scrambled out of the van, hauling on my jeans as best I could whilst trying some sort of strange rugby tackle to prevent Ci and Dog Bag getting any nearer to the approaching police car.

The car drove past us very, very slowly, with the two *gendarmes* inside giving us a very long, hard look. But they clearly decided we looked more eccentric than criminal, or they had bigger fish to fry, or, as the French say, other cats to whip, and they drove on by.

Of course it was inevitable that, on my way back and arriving at a crossroads without having a clue which way to go, I stopped in the middle of the junction and got my maps out, when the same two *gendarmes* drove up behind me. But luckily, once more, they just gave me a long look then went on their way.

After Ci had shown a different side towards men, I was hoping there were not going to be problems with him in the house when my brother was there, since my brother was not particularly good with dogs. Dogs which never bit anyone tended to bite him, although Meic was fine, never having bitten anyone in his life. My brother had even managed successfully to look after Meic and give him his essential medication when I'd had to go into hospital for an emergency appendectomy, shortly before moving to France.

I knew Ci would be fine with my friend Alex, since I've never met any animal anywhere that didn't instantly love Alex on first sight. Alex first came into my life when I had a riding centre in Wales, in the middle of nowhere.

It was known as something of a hippy safe house. Anyone needing a place to stay was welcome, in exchange for helping out around the place with whatever skills they could offer.

I already had the famous, or infamous, local hippy character, Nick the Russian, living in his converted bus on one of my fields with his lady friend. They asked me if I could find space for Alex, who needed somewhere to get his head together.

Alex had been a dairy herdsman and viewed all equines as a waste of grass his cattle could have been eating. But it was clear early on that in spite of himself, he had a natural affinity with horses and they liked and trusted him enormously. I taught him to ride and even left him in charge of all my horses, and my dogs, when I went away to do some training.

My best friend Jill's horse, Pearl, was a wonderful barometer of character. She could be a regular old cow with people she didn't like. She disliked my ex-sister-in-law intensely and once put her in plaster with a well-aimed kick. But she absolutely adored Alex.

Dogs were putty in his hands, too. I knew Ci would love him. YB was also good with dogs; his family had always had German shepherds, so a little collie would pose no problems, even a suspicious one like Ci. But my brother was a different matter. I just hoped Ci would not present difficulties and get the two of us thrown out of the Pink House.

Sensing Ci was going to have issues which needed dealing with, I'd enrolled us in the *Club Canin* in nearby Riom, and we went along for an hour each Saturday afternoon, which meant I had to get a carer in for two hours, to cover my travelling time to and fro.

I'd done dog training in the seventies with my first German shepherd, and had competed quite a lot with him in obedience competitions, though not to any very high level. But I did know the basics of teaching heel-work, positions, stays and the like.

Back in the seventies, the training methods were mostly choke chains and brute force. There was very little positive reinforcement, and titbits were frowned on. I knew times had changed enormously in the dog world so I was eager to see what lay in store for us.

The sessions we were going to be taking part in were something called *Ring*, and even after attending for six months, I never could work out exactly what it was all about. Ringcraft in the UK is about getting show dogs accustomed to the ring, to stand correctly for their breed, to trot up and down and to tolerate being handled and having their teeth examined.

Ring seemed to be some sort of basic obedience work where we walked the dogs around in a circle, but always in the same direction, periodically made them sit, lie down or stand, did a few stays then each did one recall. Nobody ever seemed to progress in these classes, although Ci and I were quickly promoted from the beginners group to the more advanced one.

Almost every dog was in a choke chain, many of them in the horrendous devices with spikes on the inside. Ci was the only dog in a harness and, perhaps not surprisingly, was one of the only dogs who didn't constantly fight to get away from his handler.

He was also the only dog there who did paw-perfect recalls every time off-lead. Some of the dogs never achieved that in the whole six months we attended. But then would you be in a hurry to run back to someone who was then going to compress your neck inside a spiked collar?

Mostly I spoke French to Ci. He was a French dog, accustomed to being spoken to in French, so I thought it fairer for me to learn the necessary commands in French than to try to teach him the English ones, humans being supposedly the more intelligent species. But for sheer convenience on the recall, I favoured the English 'Ci, come', over the French *'Ci, au pied'*, two words being preferable to three, I felt.

But no matter how many times Ci reproduced his excellent recall, with a smart present, sit and continental finish at the end, all the trainer ever did was tell me I should say *'au pied'* as the command.

And every week, we did exactly the same movement, in exactly the same order, in exactly the same place, every time. Ci started anticipating everything, glancing up at me as if to say: "This is where I lie down, isn't it?"

Worse, the trainers tended to shout a lot, especially at Ci, as he sometimes barked at other, bigger dogs, having been nervous of them during his time at the refuge. The more they shouted, the more he barked, and it was tending to make him more and more wary of men.

But I needn't have worried, he absolutely loved both Alex and YB on sight. Although it was not strictly legal, we were going to have to squash three of us, plus Ci, into my little van to head down to the Sancy and YB volunteered to sit in the back with Ci.

My brother was back for one of his visits at the same time and luckily, the presence of his two new favourite uncles had a marvellously calming effect on Ci. They became *tonton* (uncle) Alex (or Beetle, as I had always called him, from the Alexander Beetle poem by A A Milne and the song of the same name by Melanie Kafka) and *tonton* Bobby. At one point during my brother's visit, Ci even went and sat next to him, resting his chin on his knee, and allowing himself to be stroked.

The intention in taking my visitors down to the Massif du Sancy was for the stunning views. Unfortunately, the closer we got, the more it started to snow. By the time we got to Saint Nectaire itself, the sky was leaden and it was almost dark, despite being still early in the afternoon The snow was dumping down, making visibility difficult, and the roads were getting interesting, to say the least.

Our destination was a *gîte* up in the mountains, a big old hostel. If I had not had winter tyres on the van, we would never have made it up there. As it was, the last few hundred yards were a distinct challenge.

The *gîte* owners, who didn't live on site, were due to meet us there with the keys at an appointed hour. But because of the snow, and a jack-knifed lorry on their route, they were more than two hours late.

Because of my nickname of *scoot* which is how the French pronounce scout, my van was, as ever, fully equipped, so we quickly had the little gas stove boiling for cups of tea. We passed the hours by playing fetch with Ci in the ever-deepening snow.

We had the *gîte* to ourselves. As soon as we were let in and the owners had departed, leaving instructions of which pot plant in the foyer to leave the keys under on our departure in the morning, more evidence of the low rural crime rate, YB and Beetle got a roaring log fire going. I made us all a big pan of the local speciality, *truffade*, a simple yet tasty dish of potatoes, garlic and local cheese.

Another brilliant mini-break, but all too soon it was time for my "gentleman friends" to be leaving. Fortunately, with another Christmas fast approaching, I had somehow managed to persuade my brother that, as he needed to go to Brussels for some medical tests, rather than rushing back to the Pink House, he should go and spend Christmas with some of the Luxembuggers, our cousins in Luxembourg, as we all had a standing invitation to stay there whenever we wished.

So Mother and I were able to enjoy a quiet and peaceful Christmas, with Ci, who was absolutely adorable with Mother, very calm and gentle, allowing himself to be stroked by her and behaving perfectly.

Mother, of course, always called him Mikey, getting mixed up with different dogs, but since that sounded sufficiently like My Ci, Ci seemed happy enough to answer to it.

I couldn't quite persuade Ci to dress up in a Santa hat and carry Mother's Christmas stocking to her, as Meic had always done, but Meic's were big paws to fill so soon for a nervous little chap like Ci.

He seemed to enjoy his first Christmas, and it was clear that it was a huge novelty to him to have his very own presents to open. He was delighted with his new squeaky toy, though, and it filled a big void in my life to have my ears once more ringing to the serenade of a collie dog playing a squeaky toy.

Chapter Twelve
All of a Twitter

Despite being marooned at the house most of my time and escaping into the wilds on my only day off, I was managing to make new friends. As well as Lili, there was another of the carers, Emilie, who was becoming like a part of the family. Those two were far and away the best of any of the carers, better even than Hippy Chick, and I had total confidence in them and the care they took over Mother.

There were other carers, of course, some better than others, but generally speaking, they were doing a good job with Mother and I had few concerns about her care, even when I was not there.

Lili, in particular, had the rare skill of being able to learn something after seeing or hearing me do or say it just once. So it meant there was continuity in Mother's little daily routine, and on my days off, things went along almost exactly as they did when I was in charge.

Lili had a wise head on young shoulders and it was she who warned me off when a lonely and rather eccentric elderly neighbour started to befriend me. Lili informed me she was like a stray cat and once I let her into the house and fed her, I would never be rid of her.

Oh how right she was, and oh how I was later to wish I had listened to those wise words. But I've always been a softy for lonely old ladies.

It was Meic who introduced us, in fact. The woman lived in the village, but, in a way which is quite common in parts of France, because of the complicated inheritance laws which often led to land being split up and sold off at random, the little field in which she kept her goats was some distance from her house. It was the field but one away from the Pink House.

I'd already heard her strange high-pitched call to her goats as she arrived to see to them morning and evening. Having kept, bred and shown goats myself, I'd had a look at them over the fence. Although I'd started with scrub goats before going on to good pedigree stock, I found them to be a very sorry looking bunch, not in the best condition, although their owner clearly doted on them and did her best.

She often herded her goats, loose, not on leads or anything, along the road and down the cart track beside the Pink House to browse along the hedgerows. They were a bit of a handful for one little old lady on her own so I often heard her cries of: "Oh-là-là-là-là-là" as she tried to restore order and prevent them from rushing into our neighbour's garden and devouring all his plants.

Meic and I were out for a walk on the track one day when we met them head on. Meic used to have his own goats to practise his herding skills so was eager to lend a paw, but I kept him on a short lead and made him sit still for fear of sending them scattering.

We stopped and passed the time of day, as is polite in this area, and the woman asked about Meic and was he a collie and did he work sheep and so on. I made the mistake of telling her I used to keep goats. It gave us a point of contact, when I should have heeded Lili's advice and kept my distance.

For a time, we stuck to exchanging greetings when we met. Then our next door neighbour told me that the woman's only son had just committed suicide, so I felt I should offer my condolences. The opportunity arose when, seeing me in the garden as she walked past, the woman stopped and asked if I could go and give her a hand with one of her goats which had gone down and was having difficulty getting back on her feet.

I explained the situation with my Mother and that I could not really leave her alone in the house, but if it was just for five minutes or so, I would gladly come and lend a hand. It gave me the chance to mumble my condolences as best I could, not being totally sure what the correct form was for such things. But she seemed genuinely pleased and touched, so I was glad I had made the effort.

The poor goat was not looking in very good condition. To my not inexpert eye, she looked in need of a good dose of a powerful wormer and a drench for liver fluke. But as I discovered, the woman was totally hooked on all her natural remedies and wouldn't hear of anything chemical.

I'm all for the natural and the herbal but, it has to be said, there are some conditions which are so serious it's best to hit them hard and fast with something prescribed by a vet and have done with it, rather than take any risks.

But the goat lady, or, as my brother nick-named her, Goaty, was convinced her plant remedies were sufficient. Although her ignorance on the subject was alarming. All the more so as she told me she used to own and run a health food shop, selling herbal remedies to people.

One day I saw her going up to feed her goats, laden with branches cut from her garden. And as there was spotted laurel amongst her offerings, poisonous to goats, I was dubious of her skills as a herbalist. I wondered if she'd actually managed to kill off any of her customers.

We'd also heard from neighbours that she had extremely poor eyesight and was supposed to have an operation for cataracts but didn't want to leave her goats. Despite it, she continued to drive her little black Volkswagen, though it's doubtful if she could see well enough.

She clearly hadn't mastered the selection of gears. Her goat field was a hundred metres or so along the road from the Pink House, but whenever she drove away, she would whack the car into first gear there, floor the accelerator and be long past our house before even thinking about changing up. So we always knew when she was passing by the tortured screaming of her poor car's engine as it whined its way past us. Anything other than German engineering would long since have seized up under the strain.

She mentioned that she had a birthday coming up, so before I could stop myself, I found myself blurting out an invitation for her to come to tea on the day. I knew she was on her own and that she seemed to have no friends, having fallen out with most people locally, and not getting on with her daughter in law.

I should have seen the warning signs.

Another English pupil I'd acquired was a mutual acquaintance, if not friend in the true sense of the word, of Goaty, so I invited her along for tea on the same day. Mother was thrilled. She loved any excuse for a tea party and usually assumed it was her birthday.

I'd only ever seen Goaty dressed for visiting her goats, in a filthy old duffel coat, depending on the weather. So I was rather taken aback when she arrived, very much later than the appointed time, wearing an incredibly short skirt and low-cut top which looked positively racy for someone well into her seventies.

The little tea party was pronounced a success by all. I'd baked some British traditional tea-time treats, including some Welsh cakes, which all went down well. But Lili was right. Just like the cats I'd taken in, once Goaty had had her saucer of milk, she became a regular visitor to the house.

She took to calling in the mornings, just as I was trying to give Mother her breakfast and her medication, which took time, patience and concentration to make sure I gave her the correct things, and also in the evenings, on her way to or from the goat field.

Useless my trying to explain that I worked from home, often on tight deadlines, so I couldn't always just break off and talk to her whenever she wanted to. She just kept saying I needed to take a break so could stop and chat.

It also meant that she would turn up, not in her short skirt and bosom-revealing top which she wore to the tea party, but in her old work clothes, like the disreputable duffel coat, and leave a trail of straw and goat droppings, plus the unmistakable milky smell of goat, whenever she came into the house.

It was bad enough when I had Meic, in terms of the interruptions to my work and the daily routine which helped both Mother and me to get through the day. But once Meic was replaced by Ci, it was a nightmare.

Ci started out wary but all right with people. At some point something happened, and I have only a suspicion as to what it might have been, to make him decide anyone and everyone coming anywhere near me or the house, was a dangerous intruder and it was his mission in life to attempt to kill them on sight.

The Pink House had an extra door between the front hallway and the back lobby, which was always kept shut to stop Ci from attacking people whenever the front door was opened. Just as well since the carers would always knock then come straight in to see to Mother, in case I was otherwise occupied.

Whenever the doorbell rang, Ci would hurl his full, though not considerable, weight against the inner door with a frenzied barking and snarling designed to scare away any but the most intrepid of intruders.

Goaty was also keen to foist her alternative therapies on anyone and everyone, whether they wanted to hear of them or not. Her favourite remedy for absolutely anything and everything, external or internal, was *argile*, a type of clay rather like kaolin or china clay.

It certainly is a good product, I've used something very similar to get countless lame horses back on the road. But it does have its limitations – it's not a magic cure-all.

Goaty called one day to ask if I would go and help her to put an *argile* poultice on her young billy kid. As the carers were with Mother at the time so I could safely leave her, I agreed. She had been trying to poultice the top of the kid's leg, near the elbow joint, thinking his severe lameness stemmed from a twist or wrench of the joint there.

As soon as I got close enough to look, without even examining the goat, my relatively good eyes, at least with my glasses on, could see what Goaty's defective eyes could not. The cannon bone below the knee, the long main bone of the lower leg, was cleanly broken through, about half-way down its length. When I gently took hold of the injured leg, it was possible to articulate it where they should have been no joint.

I was fairly appalled that anyone could look after animals and not be able to see such an injury, or instantly identify the cause. Mercifully, she did agree to my insistence that this was a case for a vet and not for relying on a *cataplasme d'argile* or kaolin poultice.

It was because of her absolute obsession with *argile* that on one occasion I found myself physically manhandling her out of the Pink House before I did or said something I might later regret.

The degenerative joint disease, coupled with carpal tunnel syndrome, in my hands could sometimes be very painful. Like most self-employed people, I found my workload tended to be very erratic. There would either be nothing at all for uncomfortably long periods of time, or too much all at once, all with nigh on impossible deadlines.

So sometimes my hands were painful and the pain was not totally controlled by wearing my bondage strapping. Reluctantly, since I'm not usually very keen on taking medication, I'd allowed the doctor to prescribe me anti-inflammatories to calm things down a bit, since my current workload was seeing me spending many hours a day working on my computer keyboard.

Goaty, of course, was insistent that all I needed was a *cataplasme d'argile* and all would be well. Useless for me to point out that it would be physically impossible for me to work long periods on a computer, or heft my mother around, with my hands bound up in the thick layer of hardening china clay.

In the end, to stem the tide of unwanted and unasked for, not to mention totally impractical advice, I had to take her firmly by the arm and frog-march her – no pun intended – to the front door and put her outside.

* * *

Since moving to France in 2007, neither my brother nor I had gone out of our way to find and make contact with British ex-pats. We both by now spoke enough French to get by in most everyday situations, and with email to keep us in contact with old friends from home, and for me, plenty of new French friends, we didn't really feel any pressing need. It was a few years after moving to the Pink House that I discovered there was a British family living in the same area, not more than a kilometre down the road. We never did meet up with them.

But it was around this time that my long-term friend and business colleague Sarah introduced me to one of the new marvels of the Internet – social media. She told me about the new phenomenon called Twitter and being of a curious nature, I simply had to find out what it was all about.

I began by linking up to old friends and people I had known in the past, like the very annoying small boy I had taught to ride when I had worked in the local riding stables at weekends and in the evenings whilst still at school - now an adult, but still just as annoying.

With the snowballing effect of social media, I began to make more friends as friends of friends linked up. I also discovered and started dabbling in Facebook, the Dark Side, as I called it, as that took me longer to get the hang of.

Just out of curiosity, I had a look to see if there were any other ex-pats in our part of the Auvergne. By one of those strange coincidences, the one I found, a person called Christine who ran a *gîte* and *chambre d'hôte*, or bed and breakfast, about an hour from the Pink House, told me she had moved out from Marple, which was no more than a couple of miles from where I had grown up.

I suggested we should meet up somewhere, on neutral territory. Her grown-up son and daughter, both in the UK, warned her of the perils of meeting up with people you've only encountered on the Internet, but she clearly decided I was harmless enough, or at least worth the risk, as meet up we did.

As she lived near to Issoire, a town I'd visited several times and liked, I'd arranged to spend my R&R night on its municipal campsite, very close to the little hotel where I'd stayed both with my brother on our house-hunting trip and once with Meic as a special treat. I suggested we meet outside the campsite as it was a very public place, being opposite a popular fishing lake and picnic place.

That way, if either of us didn't much like the look of the other, we could just pretend a sudden interest in fishing and walk on by. Even easier for me, since with Ci in tow, I could just have been any other dog walker.

Walking around that lake with Meic had been something of a revelation to me about the attitude to dogs which predominated, in my experience, in the area and was very different to the anti-dog culture that had been increasingly creeping into the UK before I left.

Like a lot of collies, Meic loved to try to chase cars, bicycles, motor bikes, anything with wheels which passed him. It was totally non-aggressive, he meant no harm and would certainly never have bitten anyone, but he was big and bouncy.

Because of his heart condition, I always walked Meic on a harness and extending lead, just to remind him his days of running about were over. But when he saw a family walking towards us, with two small boys out in front on their bikes, he couldn't resist trying to bound towards them and then bouncing up and down and barking.

In similar circumstances in the UK, I'd encountered people telling me my dog was dangerous. To my surprise and delight, the French mother immediately told the boys to stop and get off their bikes and stand perfectly still as they were upsetting the dog.

A French car pulled up at around the appointed time for my meeting with Christine and a woman got out and started looking around. She didn't have the appearance of an axe murderer, and was seemingly unarmed, so I got out and introduced myself and, having gone fairly native, started off with the kiss on both cheeks, which didn't seem to fill her with terror.

We went off to get a coffee at a nearby place and I think it's safe to say, we both hit it off from the start and it became the start of a good and enduring friendship.

I particularly liked the fact that Christine, like me, shied away from too much contact with non-integrating ex-pats and made great efforts at improving her French. She had spoken very little when she moved out, the same year as us, although her husband Geoff was fairly fluent. To help her to learn, they didn't even have UKTV and watched French television exclusively.

I had been unable to forego my English TV favourites, although they were not many, but I'd been a long time fan of 'Coronation Street' and also loved 'Holby City' because of a totally unashamed crush on the actor Hugh Quarshie who appears in it.

Mother loved her tea parties so much I always made sure we had one to celebrate her birthdays, and now our many French friends, with Christine as the token Brit, would come along and help us to celebrate.

We could always rely on Mother to amuse the guests by reciting her poems or singing 'I'm twenty-one today' or one of her other little party pieces, as she liked to call them.

Some French are convinced that the English cannot cook. So with my conversation group, I'd taken the opportunity of putting the record straight by baking specialities from the British Isles and sharing the recipes with my students.

My signature dish is an absolutely delicious chocolate cake from Ireland with a secret ingredient which I can't tell you or I'd then have to kill you. I made it for my students and not one could guess its secret. But I did give them the recipe and they all in turn had a go at making it and we gave marks for each effort.

On one of Mother's birthdays, I decided to go the whole hog and bake specialities from England, Ireland, Scotland and Wales – Victoria sponge and seed cake from England, the famous chocolate cake from Ireland, shortbread from Scotland and bara brith, a sort of fruit loaf, from Wales.

In return they would share recipes from their own regions of France as they were not all local, so I was starting to learn more about my adoptive country.

It was Christine who introduced me to a very good way of learning about the country and its varied cuisine. 'Un Diner Presque Parfait' is the French television equivalent of 'Come Dine with Me' in the UK, where each week, five people take it in turn to host a dinner party for the others and mark each other on their efforts.

But the French version, I was to discover, was infinitely more bitchy than the British one, and the guests awarded marks not just for the cuisine but also for the ambience, as the host had to provide entertainment for them, in keeping with the theme of the evening, and for the table decorations. And as you can imagine, in a country which prides itself on its cuisine, the remarks could be scathing and the marks truly savage if high expectations were not met.

I was starting to feel very much at home, as if I was carving out for myself the new start I'd been looking for. However I didn't yet have my magic *carte vitale*, which would make getting reimbursed for medical care much easier. Every time I phoned to find out the delay, I was told that everything was in hand and the card would be with me shortly. The wheels of French administration turn exceedingly slowly.

But I had managed to successfully negotiate my way through French red tape to make sure I was paying the right contributions to the right organisations and was therefore fully legal and fully entitled to use the health service.

It had not been easy, since my profession, freelance copywriter, didn't quite fit into any one particular pigeon-hole within the system, although it exists as a profession in France, *rédactrice publicitaire.*

Luckily I never had to use the term pigeon-hole in my efforts to get onto the right system since I would never have been able to say it with a straight face since being told a funny story about the term.

Someone involved in translating an administration document had decided to take the lazy route and use an online translator, such a dangerous thing to do, especially as the translator had come up with the term *trou de pigeon* for pigeon-hole.

Now *trou de pigeon* does, literally, mean a pigeon's hole, but not anything to do with the pigeon-hole in which documents might be placed. So recipients must have been wondering why they were being told to put mail up a pigeon's bum.

It took most of one R&R to sort myself out into the right branch of the RSI, *the régime social des independants*, the social security system covering freelance workers, amongst others. I spent a forlorn afternoon in Clermont-Ferrand trotting from one branch to another, who each kept referring me back to the other, and one even told me I'd have to go to Paris. But finally I managed.

The one slight fly in the ointment to date was the discovery that poor little Ci had health concerns. He'd presented with symptoms typically associated with cystitis – increased drinking and doing mega-pees – but it didn't respond as quickly to the conventional treatment as would normally be the case so back to John Stape we went to get a series of tests done.

Ci wasn't overly fond of men at the best of times. He quickly became very 'unfond' of John Stape who had to do the unpleasant stuff like passing a catheter up poor Ci's willy to get urine samples.

Pet insurance was still in its infancy in France. When I asked at the vets, they seemed to know little about it. But I found some online which seemed good and affordable and included a package which covered things like vaccination costs and wormers, so I got Ci insured.

Thank goodness I did, as X-rays showed that he had a malformed bladder which never effectively emptied fully, leaving him very prone to repeated infections. The vet didn't want to try any surgical intervention until he had explored other options.We'd just have to live with it for now, and whenever he had a flare-up, he'd need anti-inflammatories and possibly antibiotics until things settled back down again.

Of course, it didn't greatly help his distrusting and somewhat grumpy temperament to have a painful recurring condition, poor lad.

All in all, I was happy with my lifestyle, although Mother was getting more frail, less mobile and harder to look after, with me having to lift her more and more..

But it seemed the happier and more settled I became, the more resentful my brother became. He took to telling all and sundry that I was living at the Pink House rent-free, as if I never lifted a finger around the place, and, more worryingly, telling people he was getting fed up and was going to throw me out, though he had not yet said this to my face.

He told the carers, who all reported back to me, concerned for my well-being, and even more concerned for the implications for Mother if I did have to leave. He also told his friend the ex-boxer, back in Wales, who was so concerned about me he phoned me up to see if I was all right, bless him.

It was clear we were heading for another almighty eruption, one which would make the episode of the explosive lettuce look like a storm in a teacup.

Chapter Thirteen
A Place of My Own

Once again it was the arrival of Bob and Peg which provoked the next major explosion from my brother. This time they were travelling with Young Bobby, who had now taken over the driving from his father as, at ninety-two, it was getting harder for Bob Senior to get insurance for driving abroad,

There had already been quite a few minor eruptions from my brother, usually provoked by my R&R days. My trips away were becoming more essential than ever for my health and well-being since Mother was getting increasingly difficult for me to manage and, as is so often the case with dementia, she was venting all her frustration onto me.

She no longer slept reliably through the night and often woke me up shouting, singing or laughing very loudly. She could get quite difficult when I went in to see what the problem was, demanding to be helped out of bed.

She'd also started making very determined efforts to get herself out of bed so now had to sleep in a hospital bed with cot sides, to prevent her from falling.

Our new doctor was proving invaluable as she was very kind and helpful in getting all manner of aids to make managing Mother easier for me. Thanks to the excellence of the French health care system, and armed with Mother's magic *carte vitale*, many of the items were free of charge on prescription, because they were for long-standing medical conditions.

These included the bed, which was a wonderful help. It could be raised and lowered at the touch of a button, making it much easier for the carers to get her in and out of bed, and enabling me to do so on occasion when the need arose, although I had to be extremely careful because of the ruptured disc in my neck.

We were also entitled to a wheeled walking frame for her, with a little seat so if she got tired toddling, she could just perch to recover her second wind, and a very good wheelchair. It was self-propelled, although there was no way Mother could have managed to turn the wheels with her hands. Her left hand was now permanently closed into a partial fist through a condition called Dupuytren's Contracture, and of no practical use to her.

One of the hardest things I found to deal with was Mother's absolute refusal to give me so much as a please or a thank you for anything.

Having always been brought up myself to say 'please' and 'thank you', it always grated that whenever I took her a cup of tea or something to eat, she would refuse point blank to say thank you, and if I told her she should, she would just say very haughtily: "No, why should I?"

It was an insignificant thing really but one that really got to me, and I suspected that Mother knew that and did it all the more to wind me up.

So as soon as the duty carer arrived on my days of escape, Ci and I would literally run down the garden steps, leap into the van and drive off at high speed to get away and make the very most of our twenty-four hours leave.

My brother's house had still not sold, which was understandably preying on his mind. But I was bearing the brunt of it and was increasingly coming back from my little trips to a tirade of verbal abuse, for no real reason at all.

On one occasion, I had gone on R&R the day my brother was due back at the Pink House on one of his visits from Wales. As was usual for him, he sent me frequent text messages updating me on his journey progress and I, as usual, replied, wishing him a safe journey.

Mobile phones are a marvellous invention. It's hard to imagine how we ever managed without them. But like most technology, they are not infallible, especially in rural areas with poor, intermittent signals. What I didn't know, until much later, was that the latest message from him came in two parts. The second one said he could not find his keys to his apartment so could I make sure I left the spare set, which I held, behind before I went so he could get in.

Ci and I had found a nice quiet campsite and were following our usual ritual of setting up camp and having a cup of tea before going off for our walk. Because I was busy pitching my tent – I'd been so thrilled with my little pop-up tent, I'd bought a slightly bigger one and was enjoying playing with that – I didn't check my phone to see if there was a signal. It turned out there wasn't.

It was only quite a bit later, when Ci and I went for a walk and were making our way up a long, slowly climbing track, that my phone started to beep to alert me to incoming mail and messages. There were quite a few, each getting increasingly urgent.

I phoned Hippy Chick to find out what was going on. My brother had arrived back by taxi, since he had travelled by train, so was already quite drunk. Her brother was the duty carer so he had had to deal with the explosion when my brother found out I had not left the keys as he had asked. Or rather, as he thought he had asked, because I didn't receive the second part of his message until very much later in the day; it came through amongst all the messages from Hippy Chick and her brother.

My brother was apparently currently shouting furiously, trying to kick down the door of his apartment, and raging about me, once again threatening to throw me out. And in the state he was in, Hippy Chick's brother was inclined to believe him.

Although it must have been frustrating for my brother to find himself locked out of his own apartment – but he did have his own keys, somewhere amongst his shambolic luggage, even if he couldn't find them – he was hardly homeless for the night.

There were three empty bedrooms and a shower room on the top floor of the Pink House, and the Dingley, a fully equipped motorhome with two double beds and a shower room, was parked in the garden. These facts didn't seem to have occurred to either him or Hippy Chick's brother.

So I relayed, via texts to Hippy Chick, since I was almost out of battery power and hadn't brought my charger with me just for one night away, the advice to tell my brother to go and sleep in the Dingley, in case he was in no fit state to make it up two flights of stairs to the top flat. Then in the morning all he needed to do was to phone the near neighbours, the mayor and his wife, who held a spare set of keys.

It took the shine off my little break, knowing all this was going on, and not knowing what kind of a reception I was going to get on my return, or indeed if I would find all my possessions thrown out of the house and the doors locked against me.

I did arrive back to the now not infrequent tirade of verbal abuse, and this time the threat to my face of being thrown out. I tried to remain as calm as possible and to point out that my brother was a grown man and therefore responsible for his own keys and it was hardly my fault if he lost them. And also that it was never safe to assume that mobile phone text messages, although sent, had been received.

Unfortunately, all these shouting matches were having a very bad effect on Ci. Already a highly strung little dog, and very protective towards me, he had now decided my brother was Public Enemy Number One, because he shouted at his *maitresse*. So, far from sitting with his chin on my brother's knee, he preferred to try to kill him on sight, which was leading to even more problems for me.

It was time to take stock of my life once more. I was rapidly approaching sixty years old, my current circumstances were starting to affect my health – I was getting symptoms of fatigue and feeling queasy a lot of the time – and, although I still had my little grottage in Lincolnshire, I had absolutely no desire at all to go back to the UK. I affectionately called my Lincolnshire home a 'grottage' as it had been a grotty cottage when I first bought it.

I'd signed up to take care of my mother and that's what I was going to continue to do to the best of my ability. But I had also to protect myself and my health, and I clearly couldn't continue with the current state of affairs. Time to consider my options.

To begin with, I tried sitting down with my brother to discuss things and to tell him of my concerns for my future and how difficult I was finding it to be verbally abused on a regular basis. It was never easy, talking to my brother, since he liked to talk about himself all the time, so I introduced him to the native North American device, the talking stick.

In aboriginal democracy used by many tribes, a talking stick is passed around from member to member in a tribal council circle, allowing only the person holding the stick to speak, so enabling all those present to be heard.

We didn't have a talking stick so I produced a wooden spoon and would only allow my brother to speak after I had had my say and handed the spoon over to him.

I told him that I was so concerned about the current situation that I was seriously considering moving out before I was thrown out. This would, of course, mean Mother having to go into a home. And I told my brother that he would need to be in a position to go and visit her daily since, as I had nowhere else to live and currently no means of finding anywhere, I might very well have to go back to the UK, much as I didn't want to. But I did after all have a house there still.

My house was let, and for the first few months, I had exemplary tenants who looked after it beautifully and paid their rent in full on time every month. But they then decided they wanted to buy their own home, and first asked if I would consider selling mine.

It was not something I wanted to do at that time, as it was my only bit of security. And with the housing market still at a low ebb, I knew that if I sold it, I would struggle to buy anything I liked as much for the same money at a future date.

So the very good tenants moved on, since when I'd had a succession of bad, non-paying tenants, which was costing me a lot of money and causing a lot of anxiety.

My brother was clearly shocked rigid by what I was saying, and for a time, things calmed down somewhat and he was at least largely civil.

But it had really got me thinking. I did have a little bit of money in the bank which I had been carefully saving up for a rainy day so I thought I could do worse than start to have a look around to see what was on the market in the area and what, if anything, my meagre savings might buy me.

My idea was to look for a tiny parcel of land with an old ruin or an old barn on it and start taking my R&R breaks there and potching away with my famous BIY (Bodge It Yourself) until some time in the future when I could sell my Lincolnshire property. Hopefully by then the housing market would have picked up a bit, so with the proceeds I could have a tiny little house built, as green as possible, perhaps totally off grid.

So now I was scanning the local papers and freesheets for an idea of what was out there, and even starting to go and look at a few properties. Or at least, trying to.

Estate agents here don't do too badly, since they are paid by both the seller and the buyer. And the ones I contacted didn't seem in any great hurry to try to sell me anything on their books. Perhaps they assumed that, like many Brits visiting France on a house-hunting mission, I was just a time-waster with big ideas but a small bank balance.

Twice I made appointments to view properties, cheap and cheerful small fields with barns or the remains of outbuildings. Twice I sat all alone and palely loitering, in the appointed place at the appointed time, only for no estate agent to show up. And on each occasion when I telephoned for an explanation, I was simply told the agent had forgotten our rendezvous.

I loved the area I was already in, but it did seem, looking at housing adverts, that the *département* to the North, the Allier, had much more affordable prices, so I started looking up there, though with not much enthusiasm – I missed the volcanoes. I definitely wanted a view which included 'Billinge Lump'.

On one such visit, I called into an estate agent's office to see what they had on their books and was told that, yes, they did have a property which might fit my requirements, but it currently only had planning permission for use as a weekend and holiday home.

Having just had another fairly bad outburst from my brother, I was prepared to look at anything, from a cardboard box under the railway arches upwards, so I agreed to follow the agent's car to go and have a look. My brother and I had learned on our first house-hunting visit that it needed nerves of steel and rather a lot of Valium to travel in an Auvergnat estate agent's car.

Luckily I could make the excuse of wanting to have Ci with me so needing to take my own van.

The semi-derelict building we were going to had quite a bit of rough woodland with it, several hectares, but as soon as we turned off the road and started down the track towards it, I could tell it was not going to be for me.

Down was the operative word, and I liked to be up. I loved woods but needed to be on the edge of them with open space around me and views – lots of views. This place was down in a little dell, completely surrounded by thickish woodland and undergrowth. Even if I were to cut down every single tree on the land which went with it, which I would never dream of doing, there would still be no open spaces and no views.

The house itself was small and someone had started to do it up. For some reason they had taken out the top floor completely so it was just an empty shell, tall and narrow, looking like a shoe box on end. It was hard to see where a staircase could even be fitted in without eating considerably into the quite limited floor space downstairs.

There was, of course, no electricity, water, or sanitation, and the agent, very honestly, did warn me that there was no certainty the *mairie* would ever grant permission for any. A total non-starter for me. And a very sobering experience, as it brought home to me how limited my funds were in terms of being able to afford anything, even an old ruin.

My hopes were constantly being raised then dashed, as I would find something in the paper which looked absolutely perfect and affordable. Then asking round and taking advantage of the local knowledge of the various carers, I would find the major flaw in the plan which explained why the property was so cheap.

One such place was at the nearby small town of Manzat. We had previously looked at a property there before finding the Pink House. That one had had such a large crack in one corner of the exterior walls that I would have had to block it off with chain link fencing to prevent a small dog like Ci from simply walking out through it.

The property I saw advertised was a detached cottage with a large adjoining barn, a reasonable sized garden, boasting a new roof and new double glazed windows throughout. It seemed on paper to be very cheap, so I knew there had to be a reason.

One of the carers, Marilyn - a very solidly built and competent woman, whose BO (body odour) could have killed at a hundred paces - seemed to know everyone and everything going on in the area. It was she who told me that the house stood at the entrance to what was going to be an enormous light industrial estate which had just been given planning permission, so not even worth a visit.

But it did remind me that Manzat was an area I liked and it did seem to have some more affordable properties. So on the next R&R I headed over there and went into the estate agent's to outline my requirements.

The agent told me she had the very thing I was looking for. A detached cottage in a wood, very quiet, not overlooked, in need of some work, but habitable and very reasonably priced. She assured me it was in the middle of nowhere, which sounded like my idea of heaven.

So once again I followed an estate agent's car, driven by a wannabe Monte Carlo rally driver, to go and view a very quiet cottage in the middle of nowhere.

My suspicions were immediately aroused when we had gone little more than a kilometre from the town centre when she stopped and got out to unlock a gate. I thought perhaps this was the private entrance into this remote wood she had talked about. But no. There was a driveway of probably twenty metres at the most and there was the cottage.

I'm not quite sure which part of the crumbling property the agent thought was habitable but I certainly didn't fancy the rear portion which had almost no roof at all. And as for quiet and in the middle of nowhere, there were lorries constantly thundering past on what was quite a busy road. They were so noisy I began to suspect it was them rattling past which had dislodged all the tiles off half of the roof.

The agent apologised and explained she had not been able to get hold of the keys to show me around inside but that if I liked what I had seen so far, she could arrange a further appointment to view the inside.

Mumbling my disappointment and trying to sound convincing, I said I'd phone and make a further appointment at some point, then beat a hasty retreat, feeling really rather depressed by my experiences so far.

If things with my mother and brother were getting difficult, Goaty certainly didn't help, with her constant visits and demands for time and attention. Everything from yet more help with the goats, to getting her hay crop in to removing ticks from various parts of her anatomy. She would just turn up, practically strip off and order me to take off ticks and treat the bite area with tea tree oil.

Even when I was brusque to the point almost of rudeness, she didn't take the hint that I was busy and I already had one, highly dependent elderly lady to look after. I tried to help if I could, as I knew she had no-one else to call on.

No matter how often I told her that on the evenings of my English conversation group, I was particularly busy with very little time to spare, she would turn up wanting something or another. On one occasion I was just returning from my time away and passed her on the road, driving in the opposite direction to me, heading for her home.

I was absolutely bursting for a pee, having had a long drive, so I waved but carried on driving. Suddenly I heard the familiar scream of her poor tortured VW being driven too fast in too low a gear, following behind me. She was so determined to catch me, she had done a U-turn and followed in pursuit.

I desperately tried to get into the driveway and get the gates shut before she collared me, but she came scampering up to me waving a piece of paper, something she'd seen which she thought might interest me, which was a kindly enough thought. Surely, though, she must have seen by the way I was literally hopping from one leg to another that it was not the best time for me to stop and chat.

One day she called at the house when I was away on R&R and insisted that the duty carer come and give her a hand to load her goats into her car for a trip to the vets or somewhere. I was furious, as the girls were not supposed to leave Mother alone at all, under any circumstances. Hippy Chick was even more so, as the implications, had Mother tried to get out of her chair and suffered a fall in the carer's absence, didn't bear thinking about for her and her insurance.

If my brother's attitude towards me had improved slightly after me saying I was going to go back to UK and leave him to see to Mother, it went into a steady decline as we approached the visit by Bob Snr, Peg and Young Bobby.

I had saved up an extra R&R night by cancelling some days off so I could take the visitors down to the Sancy and spend a couple of days showing them round one of my favourite areas. Because Peg was getting increasingly frail, we wouldn't be camping, but I had booked us all into a very nice chalet on the campsite where Meic had enjoyed his last night.

They arrived on a Friday evening and we had a rather fraught meal together, with my brother very much the worse for wear and being argumentative.

Peg was a staunch catholic and my brother had found the times of Sunday services at the cathedral in Clermont-Ferrand and was proposing they went.

It was a kind thought, but took no account of the practicalities involved in getting Peg, who was also now reliant on using a wheelchair, into the centre of the city and into the cathedral. Because he never took Mother anywhere on his own he was not really aware of how much effort was involved. YB was dead against, since he was the one who would have to do all the heavy lugging of his mother and the chair. He put his foot down and said no. My brother went into a wine-fuelled decline.

Whenever YB visited and my brother was there, he always liked to make a big thing of taking him out for a meal, and proposed taking him out the following day. It was a nice enough gesture, and YB did enjoy his food. But the payback was, of course, YB had to do all the driving whilst my brother did all the drinking. He also, increasingly, had to sit and listen to my brother ranting on about me and how he was going to throw me out, which YB was not at all comfortable with. He really didn't want to go out and leave his parents, as it was their holiday as much as his. So he politely declined the invitation to go with him.

My brother was beside himself with fury. He absolutely had to go out, he said, there were important things he needed to buy but he was too 'ill' to drive himself. In the end, Bob Snr very kindly agreed to drive him and off they went.

Some time afterwards, I answered a phone call and it was my brother, simply demanding, in a very brusque and aggressive way: "Where's Bob?"

Having a father and son with the same name in the same household always leads to confusion. I have always called Young Bobby by the name Bobby, which he says he prefers, and his father by the name Bob, so I can at least differentiate between them. But I was not clear what my brother meant, since presumably Bob Snr was with him, so I thought perhaps he wanted to speak to YB and offered to go and find him.

I nearly got my head bitten off. It turned out the Bob he wanted was Bob Snr, his chauffeur. He said he had left Bob to park the car at the shopping centre while he went to make his purchases, then when he came out, he couldn't find him anywhere. Quite what I was supposed to do from a distance, I wasn't quite sure but, as usual, it sounded as if I was getting the blame for it.

My main concern was for Bob. His mental faculties were as sharp as ever, but he was, after all, ninety-two and in a strange place. I wasn't even sure he could find his way back to the Pink House, if he failed to meet up with my brother.

I was most anxious that Peg should not get wind of what was going on. She was also showing early signs of dementia, and one of its manifestations was to make her extremely anxious if someone from her entourage, especially her husband, was out of her sight for any length of time.

At the moment she was happily sitting with Mother chatting away, no doubt about Billinge Lump and the thieving pickers. YB was sitting in the same room, his nose as usual buried in the latest Wilbur Smith novel. I managed to attract his attention to come into the kitchen so I could tell him what was going on without Peg or my mother thinking anything untoward was happening.

Pointless either of us taking my van or the tuk-tuk and going in search of the missing persons, since I didn't know which particular shopping centre they had gone to, and the two nearest ones were very large, so we could easily miss them. YB tried ringing his father's mobile but got no reply and I had the same lack of success trying to call my brother's.

Just as we were debating what the best course of action was, we heard a car pull up in the driveway as the wanderers returned. Bob was blissfully unaware of the anxiety, not having known about my brother's phone call. My brother was in a perfectly foul mood, as if he were the injured party. I was furious that he had not had the consideration to phone again to reassure us that all was well once he had met up with Bob, who had simply parked in a different section of the large car park.

My brother was clearly still angry that his plans to take our visitors into Clermont the next day had been voted down. YB pointed out that his parents were looking forward to spending time with Mother, as they had known her for years. I said it would be unfair for everyone to go out and leave Mother and me once more home alone like Billy No Mates, and Mother was certainly not up to a visit to the city.

My suggestion was that we should all go up to the lake at the Gour de Tazenat and take a little picnic, picnics being Mother's favourite activity of all. So the next day we got ourselves ready to do that. My brother hadn't appeared, clearly being in no fit state, but he did come out just as we were getting ready to leave, me in my van, because of Ci, the others in their car, and ask, somewhat forlornly, if he could come along.

I think we'd all had quite enough of him by this point so we drove off, claiming there was no room in either vehicle. It was probably unkind, but none of us wanted the day spoiling, especially for Mother and Peg, by his black mood.

We passed a pleasant time, and by the time we returned, my brother was asleep in a garden chair on the patio and had clearly been drinking again. Everything about his posture showed seething anger under the surface.

It was very unfortunate that, in order to get into the house, I had to walk past him with Ci. Ci sensed the latent aggression and immediately launched at my brother's feet, barking and snapping, though not making contact.

My brother woke and started to shout abusively at me, saying he was going to call the police and get them to shoot my dog, and that I could f*** off out of his house. The more he shouted and raged, of course, the worse Ci became, despite me trying to stay calm, reason with my brother and pacify my dog.

Luckily YB was there to defuse the situation and calm things down. Ci was beside himself and I was shaking, really not knowing if this time, I was about to be made homeless.

It was just as well we were all going away for a couple of days the following morning. It gave the dust time to settle and hopefully, when we got back, I would still have a roof over my head.

As usual, after such a major outburst, my brother made no mention of it once we got back and things settled into an uneasy form of normality. Then a couple of days after our visitors left, my brother decided to walk down to the shops, a trip of about three miles, as he was still too 'ill' to drive, and simply disappeared.

It was a Sunday, so not much was open. The little supermarket where he'd gone closed at midday so when he hadn't returned by late afternoon, I tried phoning his mobile but it went straight to voicemail.

When the evening carer came, I took Ci out for his walk and headed off in the direction from which my brother would normally have returned, but there was no sign of him. And there was still no sign by the following morning, with his mobile still not accepting calls.

It was my day to go on R&R and I needed to go as part of it was to be a visit to a different clinic about my painful hands, which I was anxious not to miss. On my way, I called at the local *gendarmerie* to report my brother missing.

He was, by now, becoming well known to the local *gendarmes*. One of them said he had seen him the day before, drinking at a bar in the town. They didn't seem unduly concerned and were of the opinion he would turn up in his own time.

It was that evening, when I was pitching my tent, that my brother phoned me from hospital. According to him, as he had been walking back, he had experienced excruciating pain in his back and collapsed to the floor. He had sustained a back injury a short while before when he'd been drinking at his house in Wales and had fallen down some concrete steps. In typical fashion, he had not followed any of the medical advice on wearing a back brace whilst the injury recovered, so it still gave him some trouble from time to time.

He said he'd phoned an ambulance to collect him and had then asked the hospital to phone me and inform me where he was, but for some reason they had failed to do so. I asked the obvious question: if he was capable of phoning an ambulance for himself, why did he not at the same time phone me to let me know what was happening?

Apparently, it had simply not occurred to him.

These endless mind games and dramas were getting very wearing. I needed to find my own space, even if it was just somewhere of my own to go and camp on my weekly R&Rs. Time to step up the search for a place of my own.

Chapter Fourteen
Duty of Care

So far it had been all plain sailing with Mother's carers. Inevitably, there had been a few occasions when something had gone wrong and no carer turned up, or not at the appointed time. It happened once on a Saturday afternoon when Ci and I were still going to the dog club. But as my brother was in residence at the Pink House at the time, he said he would sit with Mother for the two hours of my absence, which was a first.

I didn't think she could come to too much harm in just a couple of hours, so I went and left them to it. Although as my brother's idea of amusing her had been to do his opera practice in front of her and she'd never been very keen on opera at all, even when professionally sung, I think she was unusually pleased to see me back.

But the wheels started to come off the care package when the two very best young carers, Lili and Emilie, both went on maternity leave at the same time. Those two had been instrumental in making sure *le planning*, or the rotas, worked seamlessly. As soon as they were no longer there, it was glaringly obvious how important their input had been.

I'd had reservations over Hippy Chick's brother – let's call him Daniel - since the first occasion with the baby alarm. The problem was, since, by definition, the night carer was only there when I was not, I had no way of checking up that they were doing a good job. Mother was always fine on my return, there was never anything to indicate problems, but I had my suspicions.

But I was surprised to hear one day that Daniel was in hospital with a flare-up of his multiple sclerosis. I was not aware he had such a condition. Not an illness about which I know very much at all. But it did seem that if it got bad enough for him to require hospitalisation, and on this occasion, to have lost some of the use of one side of his body, was he the right person to be the sole night carer for my frail and vulnerable mother?

Hippy Chick was very reassuring. She said Daniel was well up to the night shifts, very experienced and if he became unwell he could immediately phone her and she would replace him if necessary. I was the last person to want to discriminate against someone on the grounds of an illness or disability, so I had to content myself with her assurances.

It's difficult having people in your house and having to trust that they will respect your wishes and instructions. Always much worse, of course, when they are there in your absence, so you really don't know what is going on.

On occasion, before I moved to France, I had had to leave my beloved Meic in the hands of strangers when I went away. Once, when working as a journalist investigating the murky world of off-shore finance, I'd had to fly to Stockholm, supposedly for the day, for a meeting with a whistle-blower. I say supposedly as my colleague, who was travelling with me, and I hadn't fully appreciated just how far from the city the airport into which we were flying with our cheap flight was located. So we missed the return flight by the skin of our teeth and had to stay overnight.

Luckily, I'd booked the dog-sitters I was using, from the utterly brilliant Animal Aunts, for two nights, just in case. They came the day before my early departure, to get to know Meic. A delightful older, retired couple, they were to look after Meic until my return. Meic was a relatively easy dog to care for, as he was wonderful at taking his medication on command. The only problem was if he had one of his psycho-motor seizures, as they could be a bit alarming to see for the first time.

As soon as the couple arrived, the woman told me that clients often got two carers for the price of one through Animal Aunts and that she was the brains whilst her husband, Brian, was the brawn.

Being a compulsive list maker, I'd made copious notes of every possible thing I could think of to cover all eventualities with Meic. But she still managed to surprise me with her own searching questions and detailed contingency plans. She made more notes and I was filled with reassurance that my boy was going to be very well taken care of.

I'd explained that as I lived in the middle of a farm estate which reared game-birds for the lucrative shooting parties they held, Meic needed to be walked on the lead to avoid problems with a very vigilant gamekeeper. I watched Brian take two very solid turns of Meic's long lead around his wrist and set off for a practice walk with him before I left. I knew I was leaving my precious dog in safe hands.

The company had assured me that their purpose was to replace me exactly, to provide continuity for the animals and follow their normal daily routine exactly. Whatever the customer wanted doing was done, including allowing spoiled pets like mine to sleep on the furniture. I knew that if I asked them to sing Meic to sleep with a lullaby and kiss him on the nose, it would be done.

I came back from my trip to be presented with what looked like an end of term report from an expensive boarding school, carefully noting everything that Meic had done throughout my absence. They were so brilliant I used them again when I went to visit Canada.

Unfortunately, although carers like Lili and Emilie, and some of the others to a lesser degree, also showed the same respect in standing in for me in my absence, the same could not be said about Hippy Chick's brother. There was an incident involving the cats during one of my absences which really annoyed me as it demonstrated, to my way of thinking, disrespect and a complete disregard for clients' wishes.

The road outside the Pink House was not particularly busy, apart from little flurries morning and evening. But for some reason it proved utterly lethal to cats. We had already lost sweet little Blackie – the neighbour across the road came to the door one morning carrying her still warm, limp body. She was probably hit by the school bus, since it was the usual time for it to pass and it did so at speeds I would have thought terrifying to its load of young passengers.

Blackie was followed in quite rapid succession by two young feral black cats who had been hanging round and who were so indistinguishable the one from the other they were simply known as Panther I and Panther II. Blackie's daughter, Barcelona, who was always quite wild, had moved on to live elsewhere, not, I hoped, a victim of the road, since I never found her body. I would occasionally see a passing black cat when out walking which would pause to look at me and Ci rather than running away as a truly feral cat would.

Mathilda couldn't be let out because of her feline leukaemia so I'd built a large outdoor run in the garden with my formidable bodging skills. It included a sort of princess tower, since I know how much cats like to climb. A thing of beauty it was not, but it was functional and Mathilda could divide her time between the house and her other accommodation, which I called the Winter Palace.

The other of Blackie's kittens, Freddie Mercury, had grown into a beautiful and imperious cat with piercing sapphire blue eyes and a withering stare. She was now known to all as HRH the princess Freddie, or just HRH, because of her regal ways. I couldn't bear the thought of her getting squashed on the road so had decided to keep her in, too.

Hippy Chick later took Mathilda to live with them as her son had met her and fallen in love with her. I had always been worried about the practicalities for me of keeping a cat with serious health concerns, which could possibly need endless trips to the vet, sometimes urgently. With me being partly marooned at the house, having to look after Mother, I couldn't always just drop everything and go. So it was an ideal solution.

So HRH was now an only cat and seemed very pleased with that status. When I was at home, I would walk her on a little harness up the garden to the Winter Palace by day and back to the house in the evening.

Her Siamese genes were strong and she refused to allow herself to be touched by anyone other than me, and that was very much under sufferance. So when I was away I left her in the kitchen, with signs on all of the doors around reminding the carers to keep them closed to prevent her from getting out. Apart from her adventure early on as a very small kitten, she had never spent a night outdoors in her life.

When I got back, Lili met me at the door, looking decidedly worried. She told me that some time in the twenty-four hours, HRH had disappeared from the kitchen and she couldn't find her. She had noticed immediately on arrival that HRH was not in her usual place, and a search of the house had not revealed her anywhere. Worse, the window to my bedroom, where the duty carer slept when I was away, was wide open, and so were all the interconnecting doors.

It was the newest and youngest of the carers, another Aurelie, who had been on duty the previous afternoon, and Daniel had been there for the night. Although Aurelie was not as hard a worker as Lili or Emilie, I had at least found her to be honest. If ever anything had gone wrong, a piece of crockery broken or the like, she always told me as soon as she saw me and I appreciated that. I intensely dislike being lied to.

Lili had phoned her immediately and Aurelie had assured her that she was positive that HRH was in the kitchen when she left. Although it was impossible ever to be one hundred percent sure as HRH often showed her disapproval of my absence by hiding away in inaccessible places until I got back.

My money was on Hippy Chick's brother, especially when Lili told me of his reaction when she pointed out that the cat was missing. It was a case of: it's only a cat. Cats go off, they always come back.

He may have been right. But that was not the point. The house rule was that HRH was not allowed out, and I expected such rules to be adhered to in my absence.

Lili was so concerned she stayed longer than her appointed time to help me find the missing HRH. By walking all round the garden and calling her, I was finally rewarded with the sound of pitiful mewing and a very disgruntled HRH appeared from under a viburnum bush, where she had clearly spent the night.

Once our favourite girls went on leave, it was clear exactly how much they had done to ensure that everything ran like clockwork. With Daniel in charge, it was catastrophic. Carers would find themselves down on the rota to start a shift with another client at exactly the same time they finished with Mother, despite there being at least a half-hour journey involved between the two houses.

I tried to stick to a routine with Mother, especially for all the medication she had to take, some of which had to be taken after meals. If she was late getting up in the morning, it meant her morning medication was late, and then got too close to her midday medication.

It had always worked very well up to now; the morning carer usually came about nine o'clock and our daily routine was based around that.

Now, however, I never knew which carer was coming or what time they would turn up. It could be anything from eight o'clock, which was far too early, Mother was barely awake and functioning, to ten o'clock, which meant she had her breakfast late and her morning medication even later.

It also meant I could not continue to do as I previously had, book a quick appointment with my doctor or dentist in the slot when the morning carer should be there, to save having to use up my precious R&R time on such things.

I didn't want to start giving Mother breakfast in bed as, even with the hospital bed to sit her almost upright, it didn't help her digestive problems and her hiatus hernia, to eat in bed. Also, as we were paying a lot of money for the part of the care package not funded by Mother's allowance, I felt we had a right to dictate terms, to a degree.

Hippy Chick had invested in a PR person for her small company, which seemed rather an extravagance to me, who was busily ringing round all the clients to arrange a visit to introduce herself and to listen to our feedback on the service.

We'd just had an incident with the carer who'd done both the afternoon and the following morning shift during my absence. Despite supposedly being a qualified health care assistant, she seemed to have made a total mix-up with Mother's medication and failed to give her any of her evening medication, particularly the sleeping drops which helped her to settle for the night. As I left very clear detailed written instructions for her medication, I found it incredible that anyone, let alone a qualified carer, could have made such an error

So although I was careful to praise what was good about the service, I did take the opportunity to voice my concerns over the rota and to point out the adverse effect it had on maintaining a settled routine for Mother.

The young PR person listened attentively, nodded in all the right places and seemed to take on board everything I was saying. I might just as well have been bumping my gums in the wind for all the difference it made. Things went on exactly as before, with the rota in a state of utter chaos.

And I had another problem to contend with. My brother's house in Wales was very shortly to be put up for auction once again, having previously failed to attract any bids at all. This time the reserve price was such that there was a very good chance that it would sell. This meant that in a relatively short time, he could very well be taking up permanent residence at the Pink House.

Time for me to redouble my house-hunting efforts, to find a safe bolt-hole, should the need arise.

So far my brother had never been physically violent towards me, just verbally abusive and threatening, but I had no way of knowing if he ever would be. I think our very nice lady doctor, who was always so kind to Mother, suspected he already was.

When my brother bought the Pink House, the *décor*, especially in the sitting room, was over-powering, over-patterned seventies wall paper that made the room look small and dingy. I decided it was time for a makeover, and, so my brother could choose his own colour schemes, I thought the best thing would be first to strip off the quite horrendous wallpaper, and paint everything white.

It made such a big difference in the sitting room that I moved on to do the entrance hall and the rear lobby. I had the aluminium steps out and was standing right on the top, on the little platform, to reach a particularly tricky bit when there was a loud crack and the steps collapsed.

Most floors in this part of France are ceramic tile, and therefore hard. My first brief sensation was of my hip hitting the tiles, then various other bits of me landed across the steps, and finally, the left side of my face hit the floor with such force I swear my head rebounded up again.

To say it knocked the wind right out of me was an understatement. I couldn't even work out to begin with whether or not I was hurt. Very gingerly indeed, I rolled slightly to get myself into a better position to attempt to stand.

Mobile phones are such wonderful inventions. They mean that when accidents befall someone alone in a house, help is only a quick phone call away. Unless, of course, they are plugged in to recharge, well out of reach by someone like me, lying on the floor in a crumpled heap. Silly tart.

Ci was absolutely brilliant. He rushed over and lay very gently across my chest, effectively pinning me to the floor even if I had felt ready to get up, which I didn't yet. He kept carefully nuzzling my face, clearly remembering his first aid training: immobilise and reassure the patient, maintain their body temperature.

But at some point I was going to need to move as Mother would need attention and besides, ceramic tiles are very cold and hard to lie on for any length of time. Gently easing Ci off my chest, I began experimentally to move various bits of me. I was getting plenty of ouches from my body, but nothing seemed too drastic, except my left arm, which refused to do anything much, and I couldn't make a fist.

I knew it wasn't broken so suspected I had just banged a nerve, probably on the step-ladder, and figured the feeling would return in due course. A glance at the step-ladder showed me that the metal retaining bars which locked it into position when open had snapped, due presumably to metal fatigue.

I very seldom bruise. I've had various falls from and kicks by countless horses that have not left so much as a mark. I also tend to heal very quickly, so I limped on as best I could, although by the time the evening carer came a few hours later, I still had little feeling in my left arm and almost no use of it.

The next day I was very stiff and sore. No signs of bruising to speak of, although I had the pattern of the step-ladder treads clearly imprinted down my left leg where I had fallen across it. By the day after, even I was turning some very fetching shades of black, blue and purple.

I already had a doctor's appointment for the following day, just for a repeat prescription of the medication for my arthritis, so whilst I was there, I took the opportunity to mention my injuries, in particular my left arm, which was still not fully functional.

The doctor was all too well aware of what my brother was like. She'd had occasion to see him at his worst more than once. As I showed her the now considerable bruising on my arm, which looked as if I'd been slammed into a wall, I could see her mind racing, considering what might be the cause of such injuries.

I hastened to reassure her and explain about the broken step-ladder. She said the arm was almost certainly a knock to a nerve which would recover in time. She said the bruising was bad and prescribed me some arnica for it.

I didn't think the bruising on my arm amounted to much so asked if she would take a look at my leg, which was truly impressive. Fortunately, the marks from the steps were now fully visible in glorious technicolour all down my left leg, so bore out my story.

As my brother's house was going to auction, it had the advantage of the sale being 'as is'. Whatever state the place was in when the hammer fell was what the purchaser would get. The vendor had just a couple of weeks to clear out whatever personal possessions they wanted to keep, but there was no need for any cleaning or tidying.

Just as well. We had made some inroads into the chaos of the place when I lived there for six months before moving out to France. But my brother had now been on his own there, off and on, for three years, and I could only imagine what it would be like once more.

So once he moved out and no longer had a fixed base in the UK, he would be spending most of his time at the Pink House. I desperately needed somewhere I could go to if things went badly wrong.

He still had his bus in an off-road storage facility in Herefordshire. Yes, correct, bus. A red double-decker London bus, a Leyland Routemaster. We'd each inherited a bit of money when Auntie Ethel, Mother's older sister, had died. Mine had sat all this time in a bank account and would now, hopefully, pay at least a deposit on somewhere for me to live. My brother had spent his on a double-decker bus.

In the early days of my dreams of a future life in France, I'd loved watching the various programmes like 'A Place in the Sun'. In it, aspiring buyers of property abroad were taken and shown various properties which either nearly matched their criteria or were so far off the mark one wondered if the researchers had been listening to the same people as we the viewers had.

There had been one episode I remembered well, with property in the Livradois-Forez, a regional natural park, along the eastern edge of the Auvergne and into the neighbouring region of Rhône-Alpes. Prices in that area had seemed to be very reasonable and it was a very attractive region, so I decided to start having a look at what was available there.

I'd discovered the French website *leboncoin.fr*, online small ads for everything from toys to houses, so was trawling through that on a regular basis, as well as estate agents' adverts.

My means were limited, to say the least, so there was not very much within my price range. I thought I'd spotted one possible, a small bungalow, which I wasn't overly keen on, but beggars can't be choosers.

It had a largish garden and in typical local style, was built above a garage with some utility rooms. It looked just about roomy enough for my needs, though it was very small. It was cheap, though, but when I phoned the agent to enquire about it, I discovered why it was cheap. It was apparently only half of the bungalow which was being sold.

From the online photos, it was impossible even to see how such a tiny shoe box of a place could be divided into two, so clearly it was a non-starter.

Then I came across something which looked distinctly possible. The location looked rural and although I didn't really know the area at all, it was roughly halfway between the towns of Thiers and Ambert, both of which my brother and I had visited previously and liked.

It appeared to have a new roof and to have been recently re-rendered so it was the same very popular pale pink colour which we had thought the Pink House was going to be, from the agent's photos.

Best of all, it had a reasonable parcel of land attached to the property, as not all rural French houses have adjoining gardens, plus there was a generous piece of land just across the road. I wasn't keen on being too close to a road but the house was built at ninety degrees to it and looked to be a little way back, so I thought it was worth a visit.

On my next R&R I found a campsite quite close to the property, at Aubusson d'Auvergne, then went exploring, to try to find out for myself where it was. As ever here, the vendor, although it was a private sale, was not giving much away in the advert as to its location.

Armed with the printed out advert and photograph from the Internet, I found a nearby *mairie* and asked them. In rural areas, everyone knew everyone and the lady on the desk was able to give me instructions to find it.

As I drove along a quiet road, I could see the little pink cottage ahead of me and my first thoughts were: 'it's close to the road', and 'it's a semi' which was not made clear in the description online.

But the location was to die for. Stunning uninterrupted views west to the Puy de Dôme and several other volcanoes, the Massif du Sancy further south, and distant glimpses of the Massif du Cantal further still. And it was a back-to-back semi, so was not overlooked at all by the other half, and it was directly south-facing, with the other house to protect it from the cold north winds.

Do you believe in good omens? The house was in a little hamlet, less than two dozen houses, which was called Le Mas. *Mas* is a southern French word for farm. The house itself sat on a plot of land called *Le Mas Sud*, south farm.

My grottage in Lincolnshire was called South Farm Cottage and was in a little hamlet of less than two dozen houses.

Moreover, with the exchange rate as it was, if I managed to haggle very hard on the asking price, I could get Le Mas Sud for more or less what I had paid for South Farm Cottage nearly fourteen years ago, and with much more land and a big outbuilding.

Le Mas Sud was being sold by two men, neighbours with houses on the far side of the hamlet. They were called Alf and Bert, which made them sound rather like gangsters. I was to meet Alf, who had the keys and would be showing me around. I had got there a bit early so I could have a look around myself first, to get a feel for the place. And I was liking the feeling I got.

Alf duly arrived, punctually, in a taxi which he was driving. It turned out he owned the local taxi firm. I'd been chatting to a very inquisitive older woman in the next door garden who told me she was the mother of the person who could become my new neighbour. She said there had been a young Dutch couple very interested in the house who had gone away to get estimates done but had not been seen for a while.

I knew from the online description that the house would need a lot of work. But then the Lincolnshire grottage had been described as 'unfit for human habitation' when I first bought it, so I wasn't easily scared off. Alf told me there was no water or electricity connected, although the infrastructure was there for both, and no septic tank. Of course, there was no telephone, but he did assure me there was broadband availability in the hamlet, essential for my work.

The front of the house was exactly as a child might paint one – two windows upstairs, a front door downstairs with a window on each side of it. There were shutters downstairs but none to the upper floor windows. There was a large attached barn which looked bigger than the house itself.

Alf unlocked the rickety front door and stood aside to let me enter first. Well, I thought to myself. Blank canvas.

It was certainly that. The door opened onto what had clearly been a kitchen of sorts. There was an old ceramic sink in one corner, bizarrely not under the window to take advantage of the lovely view and the light. There were a few old chairs scattered about, and, as Alf helpfully pointed out, a couple of sweeping brushes for making a start on cleaning up.

French houses, except possibly in the north, are not designed to let in much sunlight as it can get very hot, so this was a bit dull and gloomy. The effect was not helped by it being painted a sickly pale green colour, the sort often found in hospital corridors in the mistaken belief it is somehow soothing.

Off the kitchen to one side was a small and narrow room described as a bedroom, since older style farm properties didn't go in for sitting rooms. The occupants were either working, eating at table or sleeping. This looked even darker and more dingy as it was painted a deep shade of turquoise-blue. It would have looked perfect in a hippy squat.

Up the narrow and rather woodworm-ridden stairs, to the left was a decent sized bedroom overlooking beautiful big broad-leaved lime trees adjoining the garden. To the right was a curious small room, with a tiny slit window overlooking the landing, and next to that, another decent sized bedroom. There was not much ceiling left in any room, but it did at least allow me to see there was attic space above, and a seemingly very well built new roof.

We moved on to inspect the barn, which didn't have a new roof, although the one it had didn't seem to be in bad repair, apart from some signs of a leak in one corner. There was some ground floor space, presumably for parking a tractor, a spacious upper hay loft with an old cowshed underneath, and the essential French *cave* or cellar, which was underneath the sitting room. The barn would have been fabulous to restore and convert into the main dwelling, but such a project was way beyond my limited funds.

The land in front of the house was a decent size but totally wild, with just cow parsley and long grass. And across the road, what Alf described as the old orchard, was a long, narrow, pear-shaped strip of land which was totally wild, apart from a few straggly damson trees, which were fruiting.

It was a massive project. It was going to be a positive money pit. It would need far more money spending on it than I had or could realistically hope to have in my lifetime.

I loved it. I wanted it. I had to have it.

Chapter Fifteen
So Near Yet ...

It was now a race against the clock. In just a few short weeks, my brother would be back at the Pink House full time. I was desperate to have somewhere of my own, to escape to on my days off, so that he no longer had the power over me to make me homeless.

I couldn't walk out on Mother and I didn't want her ending her days in a home where she didn't speak the language. When she was in care homes and nursing homes in the UK, and even in hospital there, she had had endless episodes of dehydration and frequent UTIs (urinary tract infections). But since moving to the Pink House, where I could monitor her constantly, she hadn't suffered a single one of either, and her health had been remarkably stable.

However, knowing that I was no longer dependent on him might make my brother less likely to threaten me with eviction if he thought I might just call his bluff. At least, that was what I was hoping.

I didn't just want anywhere. I wanted Le Mas Sud. Not just because of all the portents but because it was the perfect place for me and I knew that anything remotely comparable in the UK would be at least five times the asking price. And I was confident that with my haggling skills and in a very flat market, I could knock the asking price down a good bit.

So another appointment was made, this time with Bert too in attendance. I'd taken the unusual step, for this area, of getting a survey done on the little grottage in the meantime. Unusual in that very few French buyers bother getting one done, taking the much more philosophical view that if a house had been standing for X number of years, it was probably good for a few more.

I used the same surveyor who had done the report on the Pink House for my brother, although, as he was from outside the area, it was not cheap. But I considered it money well spent, as when I met Alf and Bert, I could wave a document in English at them, exaggerate the faults it revealed and be confident that they wouldn't know any better.

The report was more favourable than I feared, although it stopped a long way short of suggesting I should buy. In fact it hinted strongly that such a decision should not be taken lightly.

Having looked up all the relevant words in French, I knowledgeably pointed out to Alf and Bert bulging gable ends, evidence of subsidence in some walls and twisting of the main wooden roof structure. Although because of one of my famous mix-ups of French words, this time *charpente* and *charpentier*, I actually said the carpenter was twisted.

Alf and Bert laughed off my every objection. There was really very little majorly wrong with the house and they knew it, as did I.

Then the haggling started, which in one sense was my weakest area. I can haggle well enough, very well in fact, but being dyscalculic, I get mixed up with big figures and was terrified of getting in a muddle and offering more than I wanted to or could afford.

I'd set myself a mental limit, based on nothing more scientific than being exactly what I had paid for South Farm Cottage. It was a private sale, so there were no agents' fees to pay, but I knew that *notaires'* fees for conveyancing were quite high and based on a percentage of the sale price. So I was more anxious than ever not to overbid.

Alf and Bert were also proposing a dodgy transaction whereby we only declared part of the agreed purchase price in front of the *notaire* and a cash balance exchanged hands under the table after the formal contracts were signed.

I wasn't opposed in principle to the idea of 'luck money', but I knew that what they were proposing was illegal. In Wales, whenever horses were sold at auction, the buyer would immediately rush over to the seller and demand 'luck money' back, usually the price of a round of drinks. It was accepted practice and an old tradition.

But what Alf and Bert were proposing would have bought a small vineyard never mind a round of drinks, so I was desperately trying to negotiate a figure I could afford and they were happy with.

I started at fourteen thousand euros under the asking price. I can't tell you what percentage that was of the price – I'm dyscalculic, remember – but it was a big chunk. Alf and Bert laughed and professed to be insulted.

Finally we met at eight thousand euros under the asking price. There was much shaking of hands all round and we all went back to Alf's place for them to sign a piece of paper agreeing to the sale in principle. I was so befuddled I still couldn't work out if I had overspent my budget, but it seemed I had just agreed to buy a little grottage in France.

And not a moment too soon, as my brother's house had finally, after four years on the market, sold at auction to the highest bidder. To the only bidder as it turned out.

The house was a big rambling barn of a place, a former bonded warehouse, and was to be gutted and turned into self-contained flats. But my brother was also gutted.

Although he wasn't particularly happy there, he was, as always, finding it extremely difficult to let go. His frequent emails to me spoke of making progress in packing everything up and getting ready to move out. Yet that was clearly far from the truth.

He'd already asked for a week extra to the completion date, telling the buyers he was too ill to pack. But he hadn't even arranged for a removals firm to clear his stuff, and he clearly couldn't arrange anything himself, nor could he do the removals on his own with his own lorry. And he had by now, fairly typically, fallen out with those who had previously helped him with the driving, even managing to alienate Young Bobby, the most placid of people, on their last journey together, by his behaviour.

There was not a great deal I could do from a distance, but as he'd yet again had himself taken off to hospital shortly before the completion date, I did at least manage to phone around and find a removals firm who could help him at short notice.

Unfortunately, he was by this stage in such a foul mood that the first removers were met with a torrent of abuse and a blazing row on the doorstep. So they went away again and I had to find some more.

There was simply no way he was going to be ready to move out of his house, and he knew it and was getting into a very bad state because of it. When completion date came, he had to leave behind all sorts of his personal possessions. He naively asked the buyers if they would pack them up and store them for him but, as to anyone but him, they would have looked like so much junk, they would probably have gone straight into the skip.

I was meanwhile spending a few of my R&Rs wild camping around Le Mas Sud, finding interesting little wooded spots to park the van and sleep in it with Ci, to start to get a feel for the area and learn our way about a bit.

Conveyancing was not going all that smoothly. The norm in France is for a *compromis de vente*, similar to exchange of contracts in the UK, followed by the *acte de vente* or completion. It's perfectly acceptable and even normal in France for both buyer and seller to use the same *notaire* to handle purchase and sale. But for purely convenient and geographically practical reasons, I'd elected to use my own, as the vendors and their *notaire* were nearly an hour and a half's drive away.

For reasons best known to himself, Alf was determined not to have a *compromis de vente* but to proceed straight to the *acte de vente*, which was extremely unorthodox although perfectly legal. Perhaps it was his roots – he was born in Spain, and maybe they did things differently there. But my extremely straight-laced and by-the-book *notaire* was absolutely outraged at the mere suggestion.

I'd chosen him precisely because he was such a by-the-book sort, and was also chair of the professional organisation for *notaires* in the area so I thought he was probably as on the level as it was possible to be. So such an outlandish idea was always going to be difficult for him.

His objection, he told me, was that it effectively left me with no guarantee of purchase. I could turn up on the day of the *acte de vente* only to have Alf and Bert say they'd changed their mind and decided not to sell.

Because I'd done my homework with local knowledge, talking, and more importantly, listening, to people I met in the area, I knew there was no other buyer in the offing. I also knew how long it had been on the market. And I knew Alf was doing up a property in Spain and desperate for cash, so I thought I was probably safe enough.

But to reassure me, Alf and Bert arranged for the three of us to go and see their *notaire* and discuss all the implications of missing out the *acte de vente*. There is no problem over sharing *notaires* in France as they don't work directly for clients, they are public officials, under the authority of the Minister of Justice.

I found her very reassuring, so I was able to tell my *notaire*, with some degree of confidence, that unorthodox or not, that was how it was to be done. A completion date was set for the twenty-first of December and I was over the moon – pun intended.

Good omens, remember? That date was unique, in that the winter solstice was going to coincide with a full moon and a full lunar eclipse, an occurrence which was not set to repeat itself for eight hundred years. With my pagan leanings, I definitely took that as a positive omen.

And if the conveyancing was not exactly straightforward and conventional, well, I was no stranger to bizarre house purchase, after my experiences over my little Lincolnshire grottage, the first property I had bought in my own right.

That grottage had been repossessed by the mortgage company as the previous owner had defaulted on her payments. She had various drink-related problems which meant she was not good at managing her day to day affairs. Because of the circumstances, the purchase had to be done on a tight time-frame, with no margin for error. We had four weeks to exchange contracts and another two weeks to complete.

I was thrown a curve ball when my mortgage company's surveyor pronounced the place 'unfit for human habitation' so would not release the funds. So I had to take an enormous gamble and send in a builder to a property I didn't yet own and might never do, to install a basic kitchen to pacify them into letting me have the mortgage.

After a nail-biting time with that, nothing else could possibly go wrong. Could it?

Just before we exchanged contracts on the Lincolnshire purchase, bearing in mind this meant I had just two weeks left in which to complete, I sat down with my solicitor to check over all the documents and particularly the diagram showing the boundaries on my future property.

My solicitor pointed to a shaded area in front of the house and asked if it was a ditch. I told her it was a grass verge, leading to the small front gate, the only access, and pedestrian only, to the property.

It seemed we had a problem. There was nothing showing that I had any legal right of way over this grass verge. Apparently, in order to overcome this obstacle, as the building society would not pay a mortgage on a property with no right of access, we had to show a common law right of access, to the effect that the previous occupant had enjoyed undisputed access over the verge for a certain number of years.

The legal phrase is *nec vi, nec clam, nec precario*, peaceably, openly as of right. In other words, skulking across the verge at dead of night so no-one saw her would not have counted. So we needed a signed affidavit from the previous occupant. Except that she was long gone and I was buying from her building society, who had repossessed the house, and had, of course, never lived in it.

Two weeks to go and the purchase of my first dream property was about to fall through because of a stretch of grass verge. Thank goodness for the tight-knit horsey community!

I knew the former occupant was horsey and had kept her horse in a stable on the farmyard opposite the grottage. I also knew the mother and daughter who now kept their horse in the same stable. So I started asking around. I finally tracked down a number for the former owner and rang her.

And rang her. And rang her. And rang her. As each time there was no reply and I kept leaving ever more desperate messages for her to contact me.

Finally, several days later, she phoned me, full of apology. She'd been away and not picked up her messages. I quickly explained the situation, that I needed her to provide an affidavit to say she had always enjoyed free access over the verge in order for my purchase to go ahead. And I needed it urgently, within the next forty-eight hours, or I was running out of time to complete.

She would, she said, be delighted to help. But there was a snag. My heart sank as she said it. She was currently at Pony Club summer camp. And as she was the only first aider on duty, she was unable to leave the site for another four days.

It must have been the only time in their history that my solicitors were asked to send a member of their staff, no doubt armed with brand new shiny Wellington boots, to the middle of a field, surrounded by pony-mad children, in order to take an affidavit. But take it they did and finally, that grottage was mine.

So if Alf wanted to do something a little different in selling me Le Mas Sud, I didn't really mind, as long as it eventually became mine.

My brother was now back for good at the Pink House. He was shocked rigid to hear that I was carrying out my threat and going ahead with buying a place of my own. It meant he was very careful to tread on eggshells around me at all times, although it didn't stop his drinking binges.

After one of my R&Rs – I was spending a lot of time up and around Le Mas Sud, peering longingly at my, hopefully, soon to be new home – he asked me what exactly Daniel was supposed to do while he covered my absence. He said when Daniel had arrived, after Hippy Chick had put Mother to bed, he spent a long time talking to his sister then went off to bed and didn't reappear for a good twelve hours. My brother said he had heard no sound of Daniel going in to check on Mother through the night.

Because I couldn't get Mother up, or lift and turn her in bed myself, I'd agreed the carers didn't have to change her in the night, as I didn't. She wore plenty of protection against any little leaks. But their role was to do as I always did, listen out for her and if she was unsettled, to go in and make sure she was neither too hot nor too cold, make her a drink if she was thirsty or generally attend to any other needs, perhaps giving her a few more sleeping drops to help her settle. And as Hippy Chick was charging us as much for the night shift as for daytime care, I expected that to happen.

Mother's nights were getting more disturbed. She would often make quite determined efforts to get out of the bed. One night I had heard her – luckily the bed creaked when she wriggled around – and had gone in to find her with both her legs and buttocks right over the cot rails. She could so easily have fallen.

The doctor came to check her over and adjust her medication to help her be more settled at night. On her advice, I left a note for the night carer to do two-hourly observations on her through the night, to make sure she did not get out of bed or injure herself in the attempt.

There was a folder for the carers to fill in and note everything that happened during their visits. On my return, I noticed that Daniel hadn't made much of an entry at all, certainly nothing to indicate my request for two-hourly obs had been followed.

I was not best pleased. I emailed Hippy Chick to find out why not and was told Daniel was experienced and hadn't felt it necessary and nor had she. Strange, then, that the doctor had.

My brother and I were starting to get concerned about Mother's welfare in my absence, and also a bit aggrieved that, with the very high rates we were paying, we were not getting the service we thought we were contracted for. We asked repeatedly for a face to face meeting with Hippy Chick. As it was her company, the buck stopped with her. But she repeatedly fobbed us off and in the end, sent Daniel himself round, with the young PR woman, for a meeting with my brother and me.

As Daniel was one of the major causes of our concern, it made it rather a difficult meeting to conduct. My brother left all the talking to me.

I began by asking if Daniel knew what Mother's medical conditions were and therefore why it was important to check on her when she was very agitated. I asked if he knew what a TIA (transient ischemic attack, similar to a mini-stroke) was, as Mother suffered from them periodically. I asked him if he knew the difference between a TIA and a full-blown stroke. I asked him if he knew the symptoms of a stroke and what action to take.

He answered no to all my questions. He had been in sole charge of my mother on my nights off for about two years now and appeared to know nothing about her or her needs. He knew considerably less on medical matters than I did, and I was not being paid as a carer. He also admitted he had never even read the file on Mother which Hippy Chick filled out for all clients.

My brother was clearly keeping quiet as he didn't trust himself to speak. I was coming very close to losing my temper. As it was, I could be just as witheringly sarcastic in French now as I was in English.

I sent several more emails to Hippy Chick asking for an urgent meeting about our concerns. She just fobbed me off by saying she had complete confidence in her brother. Unfortunately, if she did have, that more or less destroyed all my confidence in her.

Now that my brother was in permanent residence, I urged him to attend to various jobs about the place which would make Mother's life more comfortable and my life in looking after her easier.

The house was heated by a wood-burning closed grate in the sitting room. It had a glass front door, with a series of hot air vents to various other rooms on the same level. There was also a ventilation system running round the whole house, powered by an impressive looking monster up in the loft, with lots of big tubes coming out of it.

We had never found out how that worked. I only discovered where the switches were for its fan system when one of the cats pushed a button in the kitchen and I could hear a steady throbbing noise which drove me mad trying to identify it until I found the same switch.

Because of the design of the house, with Mother's and my living accommodation effectively being on the middle floor of three, all the firewood for the heating had to be lugged up from the driveway at ground level and stored outside the sitting room ready for use.

Firewood here is bought by the *stère*, or cubic metre, and the most economical load to order was ten *stères*. And that was an awful lot of wheelbarrow loads for me to push up the grass slope behind the house to stock up enough to keep Mother warm through any cold spells.

The first year I moved almost all of it myself. The second year I paid Hippy Chick's son to move some, then my brother and YB finished it off. The third year my brother had to do it by himself.

I pointed out to him that the fire drew too fiercely and it was impossible to shut it down effectively to maintain a low burn overnight. So not only was it not efficient and was using too much wood, it meant the extra work of having to relight the fire again every morning. He promised he would have a look. I said he should get a professional in.

One day when I got back from my R&R, the duty carer reported that the fire had been a bit more smoky than usual. I had a quick look but couldn't see anything untoward, so thought no more about it, other than perhaps a piece of timber that wasn't fully seasoned.

Usually in the mornings, after taking Ci out for a quick walk before Mother woke up, I would make her a cup of tea first to give her chance to be fully awake by the time the morning carer arrived. Then I would get on with attending to the fire, so the sitting room was nice and warm for her after her breakfast.

For some reason, that morning, I went into the sitting room first, and noticed that it was once again very smoky. It's a bit like the elephant in the room. Sometimes something is so big, and so blindingly obvious, that it takes you several moments to notice it.

The reason the room was smoky was simple. Although the fire itself had as usual burned away to nothing, the big wooden mantel above the inset fire was smouldering and glowing red hot and a hole was gradually appearing in the plasterboard above it. Behind the hole, the pipe from the fire inset to the chimney was also glowing an angry red.

There's a question people often pose. If the house was on fire, who would you rescue first? I'm afraid my first reaction was to put Ci safely in my van and park the van away from the house. I knew I couldn't get Mother out quickly, and to do so would have meant taking her past the source of the fire anyway, which would have been extremely dangerous. But I did shut the air vent into her room to prevent smoke from getting to her whilst we waited for the *pompiers* (firemen) to arrive.

I also woke my brother, which was not easy. He had, as was usual on my R&R days, clearly been drinking heavily. So it took a lot of hammering on his door and shouting "Fire!" to rouse him.

The *pompiers* arrived swiftly, as they didn't have far to come, and were absolutely wonderful. They said it was exactly the right course of action to leave Mother where she was, as her room was some way from the source of the fire so she was much safer there. It would clearly not have been a good idea to take a ninety-three year old lady in her nightclothes out into the garden on a chilly November morning.

Whilst waiting for their arrival, I had thrown a few buckets of water over the smouldering mantelpiece, so they soon had things under control.

But they did have to hack out all of the old fire surround and plasterboard and tip it all out on the lawn to make sure there was nothing else left smouldering, and what a mess it made everywhere.

So for the time being it had to be a portable gas fire and electric wall heaters to keep Mother warm, and I had to explain away the gaping hole in the wall as having some alterations done. Fortunately she was far more interested in all the dishy young men who were still swarming about when we got her up and took her into the kitchen for her breakfast.

With the prospect of completion of my new grottage approaching, I was going to need care cover for Mother whilst I had various meetings with vendors, *notaires* and the like. Hippy Chick was becoming increasingly difficult to deal with and increasingly inflexible over the rota.

I asked for some definite time commitment, especially in the mornings, so I could arrange meetings with my *notaire* at times when I could leave Mother for an hour with the carer. I pointed out that this was impossible for me to do if her staff constantly came at a different time each day. Her very unhelpful reply was that I should make all my appointments on my R&R days.

My brother and I decided, therefore, to try another company to cover any additional hours, so we went back to the other one of the two we had interviewed when we first arrived. I had dismissed them as I found them a bit impersonal, more interested in the paperwork than in Mother. But they did have the advantage of being considerably cheaper than Hippy Chick, and they told us they had a very reliable woman who lived only three kilometres from us, which sounded ideal.

As soon as I saw Madame LaC for the first time, I knew we were in very safe hands. She was a very large lady indeed who could have given Matron Hattie Jacques, from the old Carry On films, more than a few pounds. But she oozed efficiency and arrived exactly at the appointed time for our first meeting.

Although she spoke no English at all, she was so smiley, friendly and jolly, that Mother was soon hugging and kissing her and the two of them got along famously. She was very strong and very proficient at moving Mother from armchair to wheelchair to bed. I showed her the medication lists and she immediately took it all on board, and the same with Mother's likes and dislikes over food. I felt myself heaving a huge sigh of relief.

Best of all, for her to cover a night shift cost less than half of any of Hippy Chick's carers, and what was provided for the fee was much more. Daniel's idea of a night shift was to spend as much time as possible shut in my room, which the carers used, playing with his mobile phone and, if he remembered to plug it in, occasionally listening out for Mother on the baby monitor.

Mme LaC's firm charged two different night rates, both of them much cheaper than Hippy Chick. A *nuit calme*, quiet night, was based on them checking on their charge four times through the night. If more checks were required, they were available, at a very slightly higher rate, for a *nuit agitée*.

Furthermore, these carers did not expect to go to bed in my room. The norm was for them to catch whatever sleep they could, between checks, on the settee in the sitting room, with the baby monitor always plugged in and within earshot.

So it was with perfect confidence that I booked Mme LaC for the morning of December twenty-first, which was due to be the completion date on Le Mas Sud. It was my R&R day anyway, so Hippy Chick's carers were already booked for the afternoon, night shift and following morning.

As the signing of the *acte de vente* was set to take place at nine in the morning, Mme LaC was due to arrive at eight o'clock so I could do a brief handover to her capable hands. She would then in turn hand over to whichever carer from the other company came at two o'clock.

So by about ten o'clock that morning, I would be the proud and happy owner of Le Mas Sud and would head up there to camp out and enjoy my new home and celebrate the winter solstice with the full moon and the lunar eclipse. Perfect.

With so many positive omens, nothing could possibly go wrong. Could it?

Literally at the very last minute, I got an apologetic call from my *notaire*. Because of a small glitch on the paperwork, completion could not take place on the set date. But everything was set for it to go ahead exactly one week later.

I was absolutely beside myself. Useless to explain my pagan superstitions about good omens to my dry as a stick *notaire*. He simply said there would be other solstices, and other full moons. Yes, but never again in my lifetime the two together with a lunar eclipse.

So instead of my celebratory campfire meal at my new house that evening to watch the full solstice moon rise, Ci and I curled up together in the back of the van up at the Gour de Tazenat.

Try as I might, I couldn't lift the gloomy black cloud that settled over me and made it hard to put one foot in front of the other. It was only a week's delay but to me it seemed like an eternity.

To make matters worse, Christmas was again looming, my brother was at the Pink House, and he was going into a steady decline. Mother also was not as well as of late, so I had to call the doctor out to check her over.

My brother was in one of his dark depressive moods and kept coming into the sitting room, plonking himself down next to Mother and crying and howling, whilst holding her hand, which was very distressing for Mother.

So that when the doctor came, as well as attending to Mother, she also had to arrange an ambulance yet again to take my brother away to the local hospital, with yet another recommendation that he should go for an extended stay in a psychiatric clinic.

At least it meant another quiet and peaceful Christmas for me and Mother, watching mindless nonsense on the television and keeping warm, as best we could, by the gas fire.

And then, finally, on the thirtieth of December, the *acte de vente* went ahead. I signed what seemed like an endless pile of documents and I was at last the proud owner of a ramshackle money-pit of a grottage.

Chapter Sixteen
Thieving Pickers

My brother came back from his latest stay in hospital on January the first. But there was no sign of his New Year's resolution being to take better care of himself or to seek the professional help he so clearly needed and was constantly being advised to accept. Within three weeks, he was back in hospital yet again and once again didn't stay long enough or follow through on treatment.

Mother was getting increasingly frail and more resentful of me and my attempts to look after her. More and more, she had started doing loud theatrical sighs to get my attention whenever I left the room to prepare a meal or to try to do some work.

She kept calling for her mother. I had tried once to explain that her mother had died long ago but it upset her so much that I'd stopped doing that. Instead, I always said her mother had gone to St Helens, their home town, or sometimes I'd say she'd gone to Billinge Lump.

Mother would always perk up at the mention of Billinge Lump and say: "Oh yes, she'll have gone to get the best blackberries before the thieving pickers get them."

Sometimes, especially when I tried to move her from place to place, she would groan loudly: "God help me, please, God, help me." She'd also started to shout this in the night.

I found it upsetting. I don't personally believe in her god, and I was trying to help her, as best I could, but it seemed more and more that whatever I did was not right and not good enough.

Although she was on the highest level of attendance allowance, Hippy Chick advised me to contact the *Conseil General* who paid it to see if there were a few more coppers to be squeezed out, to help with the increasing care she needed.

Hippy Chick had started to be very difficult since we had had the temerity to question her brother's competence. It's always very tricky, in business, employing one's own family. And when they were as inept as Daniel, one had to make a professional judgement whether to continue to support them or to listen to the client and try to respond suitably to their concerns. Hippy Chick had chosen to back her brother all the way. I admired her family loyalty, but not her business sense.

Since Daniel had taken over *le planning* and Hippy Chick was refusing to meet clients to address their concerns, the staff turnover was suddenly much higher. The carers simply became disillusioned at never being anywhere on time and often bearing the brunt of the clients' frustrations. Hippy Chick had tried bringing in other family members to fill gaps. A sister-in-law did a few shifts but was worse than useless. And I was very angry on one occasion when I saw that Hippy Chick had put her teenage daughter on the rota to cover some of the night shifts.

I had been assured that the night carer would always be an older and experienced member of staff. It was bad enough to discover that Daniel knew absolutely nothing about basic first aid and couldn't even recognise the symptoms of a stroke. But to think of a teenage girl whom I didn't know and Mother had never met, as far as I knew, being left alone in charge at night was very worrying.

Again Hippy Chick was very dismissive and said her daughter had had work experience in an old people's home and was experienced in end stage care. But my point was my mother was not yet at end stage. Although she was getting frail, she was physically not too bad for someone approaching ninety-four. It was not merely a case of sitting beside her bed waiting for her to shuffle off this mortal coil.

It required someone who could recognise if things were going wrong and she needed medical intervention. And as I pointed out, we were paying full, inflated, day-time care rates, not a baby-sitting service.

A couple of days into the New Year we were due to have a review visit from the *Conseil General's* doctor, who would assess Mother's condition and make recommendations about her care allowance. It was perhaps fortuitous that I was genuinely having a bit of a carpal tunnel crisis when he called so was resplendent in sexy bondage strapping on both wrists when I opened the door to him

He asked detailed questions about Mother's daily needs and how they were met. I told him about the carers' input, explaining my difficulties in getting her in and out of bed. He asked how things were working out with the current carers so I told him frankly about some of the recent issues we had experienced.

I told him we seemed to be paying a lot for a not very brilliant service and asked him what the going rate was for night care cover. He professed not to know, saying he was not involved in that side of things.

So I mentioned the sum we were paying, for both day and night care, which were charged at the same rate, then went on to voice some of my concerns about Daniel's apparent lack of knowledge. I mentioned in particular that the night carer didn't know what a TIA was, what the symptoms of a stroke were or how to differentiate between the two.

The doctor was extremely professional and very discreet. He said very little, but as I spoke, his eyebrows began to climb ever higher up his forehead. A bit like Star Trek's Mister Spock. They climbed so high, I thought they might actually travel over his scalp and work their way down to the back of his neck.

Marilyn, of the fearsome BO, was the carer that morning, and had been getting Mother up and putting her into the kitchen in front of her breakfast, which I had prepared and left ready for her. The care book was in the living room, where I was talking to the doctor, so Marilyn came in to fill it in.

I saw no reason to stop what I was saying to the doctor, as it was nothing I hadn't already said in emails to Hippy Chick, and to Daniel himself to his face. But I reminded Marilyn that she should treat as confidential anything she overheard and that it would be very wrong of her to repeat it to anyone.

Less than an hour after Marilyn left, the doctor had also gone and I had helped Mother to finish her breakfast and given her the morning medication, I received an email from Hippy Chick. It was seething with such rage I'm surprised it didn't spontaneously combust in my email inbox.

She repeated a lot of her earlier exchanges with me, about how much confidence she had in her brother, how they knew what they were doing and were providing an excellent service. She went on to make all kinds of claims which were patently not true.

She tried to take all the credit for the improvements in Mother's health we had seen over the past four years, completely overlooking my input, which was considerable. She claimed that when Mother had arrived in France, she had been unable to walk, talk or eat. All complete nonsense, since on the trip over in the motorhome, Mother had chatted most of the way with the two nurses accompanying her. And when we had broken our journey for the night in Calais, she had sat at table with the rest of us and eaten well, although a small portion, managing to feed herself and clearly enjoying it.

Hippy Chick finished the vitriolic rant by saying that as we clearly no longer had confidence in her carers, she was withdrawing the twenty-four hour cover for my R&R days with immediate effect, so no cover for me the following day. And that with one week's notice, she would be withdrawing her care cover altogether.

So she was demonstrating her care and commitment to a vulnerable elderly person by withdrawing all care cover. Nice. And I had been trying for weeks to have a face to face meeting with her to discuss our very real concerns, since I believe in direct action rather than going behind someone's back.

The following day's R&R cover was essential as I had appointments at Le Mas Sud. There was no way I could leave my brother in charge of Mother. Even at the best of times he could not cope. And he was currently in a fragile mental state himself. But I couldn't cancel as I was starting to get estimates for essential work on my new grottage.

Through my insurance agent, I had found and joined an organisation rather like a collectivity of small businesses – apparently, even a one-person band like me qualified. It was brilliant for me as their accounts person, more a book-keeper than a professional accountant, but every bit as good, would call on me two or three times a year, go through all my chaotic scribbled paperwork and attempts at keeping accounts and sort everything out for me.

When I mentioned to the accounts person the location of my new grottage, she said they had another English person in that area on their books, who was a builder. Whilst I never deliberately sought out other ex-pats, and certainly didn't want to use only British tradesmen, I thought it would be a helpful start to have someone I could discuss my needs with, without struggling with unfamiliar vocabulary, to get me started.

I urgently needed to get the small leak in the barn roof fixed, as the water ingress was rotting the floor of the hay loft. I also needed to replace the downstairs windows soon as they were not secure, and I needed some ceilings back upstairs, to help keep the building a bit warmer and stop any problems from cold and damp. Not to mention making it more pleasant for me to camp out in, which is what I intended to be doing every R&R day for the foreseeable future. And my first appointment with the builder was for the following day.

It's in times of crisis you find out who your true friends are. Christine, the English person I'd met through Twitter, had told me she used to be a nurse. I'd managed to get Mme LaC for the night shift, but neither she nor anyone else from her agency were available for the afternoon and the following morning. Would Christine, by any remote chance, be available and willing to cover?

Since our first meeting, we'd met up a few times, been to each other's houses, done ladies wot lunch together, and generally become good friends. Christine had been to some of our tea parties, and Mother's last birthday party, so she knew Mother. She would be delighted, she said. Phew! Or, as the French say, *Ouf!*

With that vital R&R out of the way, and a very productive meeting with the builder, I could then contact Mme LaC's agency about picking up the rest of the old carers' shifts. Fortunately, they had carers available and could do so. Mme LaC was to be Mother's primary carer, covering the majority of the shifts for continuity, and there would be a couple of other regulars. It was going to work out considerably cheaper, hopefully for a better service, and they were much more flexible in picking up occasional extra shifts when needed.

And they were needed, as both Ci and I were having some medical problems so needed to make appointments at the vet and the doctor respectively. Because my brother hated ever to be outdone on medical matters, he was increasing the frequency of his hospital visits, treating it in some respects like an hotel, sometimes 'checking out' for an *exeat* day then going back in.

Mme LaC was kindness and consideration itself, not just for Mother but for the welfare of all the family. She would sometimes call in on my brother if she was passing the hospital when he was there, just to say hello and see if he needed anything.

Ci's problems were again related to his malformed bladder, which was causing more frequent episodes of painful cystitis. The vet wanted to do various procedures, including a laparotomy, to see if there might just be something he could do surgically to ease the problem. But despite having a good old root round in poor Ci's abdomen, examining his defective plumbing, he decided there wasn't and the only answer was to keep up with the anti-inflammatories whenever he had an acute attack.

My problems were a little more mysterious. I was extremely tired all the time, in a way which could not be fully explained by the frequent disturbed nights with Mother. And my once legendary appetite was deserting me, leaving me often feeling too queasy to eat.

When working as a reporter on a newspaper in South Wales, I'd gained the nickname of Desperate Dan, after a cartoon character in The Dandy comic, who used to eat cow pie, with a whole cow in it. That was because I would often have wolfed down three or four cream cakes before lunchtime.

So far the only abnormal thing which had shown up on blood tests was low ferritin, the substance responsible for the body's storage of iron. But to date there was no explanation for why this should be.

Blood tests are much easier and much more pleasant in this part of rural France, since the nurse comes to the house to do them. That's because the tests are often required to be done fasting, and no self-respecting French person would even think of leaving the house in the morning on an empty stomach, without at least a cup of coffee inside them.

I randomly saw both of our very good doctors, each of whom had their own pet theory for the cause of my problem. The male doctor wondered if they might be related to something in my new grottage, old lead-based paint or other noxious substances. The female doctor, knowing my rather difficult family circumstances, felt they were enough to explain the problems.

Neither theory really held up, though, since the symptoms were constant, whether I was at the Pink House or in the peace and quiet of the grottage. And I had not yet started stripping off any old paint or doing anything similar which might account for it.

With the changeover of care for Mother from one agency to another, we had to have a meeting with her social worker and the financial person from the *Conseil General* to sort everything out, so the transfer was done seamlessly and the carers were paid.

I'd been very impressed by the new care agency as I was required to sign time-sheets for each and every carer who came and to note exactly when they arrived and how long they stayed. Never once had I been asked to sign anything similar with Hippy Chick's agency.

Mother's allowance from the *Conseil General* was paid direct to the agency, and we received invoices from Hippy Chick to pay the balance, which was always considerable. I handed over the various invoices we had received from her recently to the financial lady. Her eyes narrowed like a hovering raptor, spotting its prey.

Hippy Chick's agency had covered just over a week of the new year before she spat her dummy and pulled the plug. She'd sent the bill for December on Christmas Eve and when my brother hadn't paid it immediately, as he was in hospital so had not received it, she had added a whopping penalty fee to the January bill, of about a quarter of the December bill. The January bill covered the hours she'd claimed for in the nine days her carers had worked.

Of course the financial lady immediately spotted what my mathematically challenged brain could not – she had actually claimed for more hours than her carers had worked. And when the finance lady started to flick back through the previous invoices, this was not an isolated incident.

When she saw the sums we had been charged over the years, it was a repeat of the ascending eyebrows episode with the doctor. Although in her case, she did not hold back in saying exactly what she thought of someone who appeared to have been milking the *Conseil General* for all she was worth.

It seemed the 'thieving pickers' as Mother would have called them, had been ripping off not just the clients but also the *Conseil General*. And that latter was not a wise thing to do.

But the good news was, there was no problem at all in transferring Mother's allowance to the new agency, and she was very pleased with the efficiency of their forms and timesheets, and scathing in her criticism of the lack of them from Hippy Chick. She would, she told me, be investigating the matter further.

And the very good news was that a few more euros had indeed been found for Mother's care package. In France, the role of a family carer in looking after elderly parents at home is respected. There is recognition that without their help, the homes for the elderly would be totally swamped.

The doctor's report had acknowledged my need for R&R in the interests of my health and therefore in Mother's best interests overall. A small increase would be made to her allowance, therefore, to help to pay carers on my days off.

My brother had decided he needed to go back to the UK to tie up a few loose ends and get some of his things from his lorry in storage near Hereford. So things were once more peaceful at the Pink House, especially with the new carers turning out to be so efficient.

Of course, as in any organisation, there were little glitches. Or rather, potential glitches, as Mme LaC proved to be a formidable organiser.

She was almost overpowering, especially with her sheer size. She would sweep in and announce that there would have been a problem with the planning but she had already done A, B and C and swapped round shifts X, Y and Z so there no longer was. Which was exactly what I liked to hear.

Mother, meanwhile, was starting to get the sort of problems which often affect elderly people and others of limited mobility. Although she ate reasonably well, her food did not always put in a reappearance as it should have done.

I had to liquidise all of her food now into thin hippy slop in order for her to be able to eat it. But although I was always careful to include as much fibre as I could, and she was also on a medical fibre supplement, the lack of exercise was slowing things down to a crawl.

I called out the very kind lady doctor, who came immediately, and gave me some real depth-charge strength medication for her, and said if she was no better the following day, to let her know.

To help with the problem, I was still trying to mobilise Mother as much as I could, even if it was only a few steps at a time. In particular, I was still trying to take her to the loo, hoping the familiarity of the action would help.

But she was getting increasingly difficult to move and she would make very little attempt to help me, just allowing her legs to buckle whenever I tried to stand her upright. On this occasion I managed to get her to the loo, where we had installed a rail on one wall and a grab handle on the other so she could use her arms, which were still quite strong, to support at least some of her weight and make things a little easier for me.

She was determined, though, not to make any effort so I couldn't get her off the loo without her falling. There was the big hoist with which we had been issued for moving Mother about in the house. I brought that to the loo and tried to use it, but she disliked it so much she always made an enormous fuss and we were getting nowhere fast.

The only thing was to do a dead lift, with her hanging onto my already injured neck for dear life, then take her back to the bedroom and put her back to bed for a rest as she was by now as exhausted with the efforts as I was.

Unfortunately I'm not a trained carer and try as I might to get it right, she did finish up half falling in my efforts to transfer her and finished up banging her shins against the walking frame I was using to try to get her to support some of her own weight. And because she had very thin and fragile skin, it split immediately.

I did some first aid to soothe and dress her legs but decided that, with open wounds on both legs and still no reappearance of the doctor's blockbusting remedy, it was time to call the doctor back.

Once again, wonderful French healthcare – not only did the doctor make another house call, she made it very swiftly in response to my phone call. She decided Mother would need to be treated in hospital as she was going to need some complicated and unpleasant plumbing procedures to put things right.

An ambulance was summoned and Mother went off for her first ever visit to a French hospital in the four years she had been living in France. I followed behind in the van so I would have transport to get back to the house.

All the medical staff were very kind with Mother. I couldn't be in the room with her whilst they were carrying out their various procedures, for which I was quite thankful, but I could hear through the door that they were all making efforts to speak at least some English to her and to reassure her as much as possible.

Afterwards they said that as it was not a very nice procedure and she was now a bit dehydrated and exhausted, they would keep her in for a little while under observation and keep her on a drip.

They kept her in for a few days, which meant I caught up on some much-needed sleep, with no more disturbed nights. I went in to see her almost every day and took the high calorie milky supplements she had on prescription, to make sure she was getting enough nourishment, as the hospital was much like any other, not enough staff to individually feed each little old lady under their care.

On the days when I couldn't go, because of appointments at the grottage to see about getting mains services and utilities connected, the wonderful Mme LaC would go, in her own time and unpaid by us, to make sure Mother got her supplements and a friendly face to fuss over her.

My brother was also now back from the UK so he, too, could go in and see her and get her to drink something.

Mother quickly perked up and was soon allowed back home. As soon as the ambulance crew delivered her safely into the sitting room at the Pink House, I asked her if she would like a cup of tea.

It was a very empathic affirmative. In fact, it was one of her famous mixed-up phrases which she brought out quite unintentionally from time to time.

"Can the Pope swim?"

She'd heard both the phrases 'Can a duck swim?' and 'Is the Pope a Catholic?' as a way of replying to a rather obvious question, and had forever muddled up the two.

As soon as she had finished her tea, I put her to bed, and managed to do it this time, as she was tired out after the journey back. I think she was so relieved to be getting back into what she clearly recognised as her own bed that she actually helped me quite a bit with manoeuvring her.

Mme LaC got her up the next morning but it was clear Mother was still very tired. She would, after all, be ninety-four in just three days' time. I managed to get her to eat her breakfast, with a lot of help from me, but trying to get her medication into her was a real struggle. She just didn't seem to want to be bothered any more and the more I tried, the more aggressive she became, slapping my hand and pushing it away.

I took her back to bed and just let her rest, going in regularly with cups of tea, some of her high calorie drinks, and anything else she fancied and I could get her to eat. I kept asking if she wanted to get up, but she kept saying determinedly: "Stay in bed", so I let her.

On the morning of her birthday, when I took in her cup of tea, we had one of our familiar conversations, although her voice was now getting noticeably weaker.

"It's your birthday today."

"Is it? How old am I?"

"You're ninety-four."

"I'm not! Ninety-four? I never am! Ninety-four my bum."

"Well how old are you, then?"

"Twenty-one!" Although this time, she didn't have the strength to sing her usual song.

The end was coming, and I knew it. Knowing how fond some of her old carers were of *la mamie anglaise*, I sent them text messages saying they should perhaps come and see her. Emilie and Aurelie came the following morning. Little Lili, our favourite, phoned me to say she couldn't bear to see Mother nearing the end, would I be terribly offended if she didn't come and just kept the memories she had of her in better times?

Of course I wouldn't be, I understood completely. Lili was the most sensitive of them all and I knew she would find it difficult. The other two came and kissed her and made a big fuss of her and Mother seemed pleased by the attention.

I called the nice lady doctor to come and advise me. Mother was now having difficulty drinking and swallowing anything so I didn't know what to do about the medication. And she seemed to have given up, she didn't really want to make the effort to take anything.

The doctor was, as usual, absolutely wonderful. She prescribed jellified water, a sort of gel that I could carefully spoon into Mother's mouth, where it would dissolve and at least give her some liquid to stave off dehydration.

Then she carefully wrote out a full prescription of all of the medication Mother was taking and next to each individual item, she wrote 'Discontinued.' I knew that this was effectively signing my mother's death warrant, as without the medication, her heart and other organs would simply fail.

Doing it that way with the prescription, which I had to take to the pharmacy to be logged onto their computer, completely exonerated me of any blame in simply withdrawing her vital medication when the fancy took me.

Mother was sleeping more and more. Whenever I could, I got her to take little sips of the jellified water or even a spoonful or two of the milk supplement, when she could manage it. We went on like that through the night and throughout the next day.

By that night, she was clearly fading. I was nearly out on my feet with the fatigue that was dogging me, but I tried to stay with her as much as I could.

She took hold of my hand in hers, with a grip that was still surprisingly strong, and began to shake my hand quite vigorously to and fro.

I couldn't work out if she was asking me to stay or telling me to go. Sometimes, even recently, in her better moments, when I'd say I had to go to do something or another, she would say: "You go. You have your own life to lead, I know that. You go. I'll be fine. Don't you worry about me."

I wasn't sure if that was what she was trying to say to me now. I thought I'd just go and catch a couple of hours sleep before I dropped.

When I came back, Mother had gone to Billinge Lump, to pick the best of the blackberries before the thieving pickers came.

THE END

About the Author

Tottie Limejuice is the pen-name of Lesley Tither, a freelance copywriter and copy editor who lives in the Auvergne region of Central France. Passionate about wildlife and the countryside, she enjoys walks and camping with her dogs, and organic gardening. Now firmly settled into rural French living, she has applied for dual British/French citizenship.

Contacts and Links

Email

tottielimejuice@gmail.com

Facebook link

www.facebook.com/pages/Sell-the-Pig-Tottie-Limejuice/

442840135795573

Blog link

http://tottiesbookblog.blogspot.fr/

Twitter

@tottielimejuice